SOMETHING ABOUT THE AUTHOR

Professor James O. Swain received his higher formal education at Indiana University: B.A. degree 1921 and M.A. degree, 1923; and the Ph.D. degree, University of Illinois, 1932. He has also studied for short periods at the University of Madrid, the Sorbonne, and the University of Chile. He has lived in Costa Rica, Mexico, Spain, and Chile as well as in France where he spent several months during the First World War. He has lectured in Spanish in Spain, Venezuela, Paraguay, and Chile. A Pan-American World Airway Travel Grant in 1951-52 gave Professor Swain an opportunity to meet the outstanding men of letters in Chile while lecturing on American Literature at the famous Summer Session.

Like many of the older generation of Spanish teachers, Mr. Swain had little formal training in Spanish American Literature, but his association with leaders in the field, especially with members of the *Instituto Internacional de Literatura Ibero-Americana,* has given him an appreciation and love for the great writers of Spanish America. Mr. Swain's introduction to Dr. Marin and subsequent conversations with him in Washington, D. C. and at professional meetings emboldened him to ask Mrs. Milena Luksic de Marin for the honor of being Dr. Marin's official biographer in the United States.

Mr. Swain was professor of Romance Languages at the University of Tennessee from 1937 to 1964 being Chairman of the Department from 1937 to 1958. He has been active in the AATS and the MLA. Besides preparing a number of language texts, Professor Swain has published articles in encyclopedias, in the *Modern Language Journal,* and in *Hispania.* He is fully retired now but maintains an office at the University of Tennessee.

Juan Marin-Chilean
The Man and his Writings

James O. Swain

LEE COLLEGE FACULTY STUDIES — Humanities

Pathway Press Inc., Cleveland, Tennessee, U.S.A.

MANUFACTURED IN THE UNITED STATES OF AMERICA

(JUAN MARIN—ca. 1952)

To

Milena Luksic de Marin dedicated wife of
Juan Marin, our author

PREFACE

When a man of accomplishment, especially when he is known to have ambitious plans for years to come, leaves this life, we cannot refrain from asking that answerless question, Why? When this person of accomplishment is also a friend, the question is, of course, much more personal. We wonder what will become of the unfinished work left on the drawing board. Who will try to pick up the scattered pieces of the jig-saw puzzle which only the departed knew how to fit together? However well a successor will continue his work, something will be lost; the bells toll for all of those who are left gazing nostalgically after the friend who has sailed away into the mysteries of the hereafter.

As a man who read very widely and felt obligated to discover and help others discover qualities to be remembered in famous men of science, philosophy, and letters whose passing was news in his life time, Juan Marin left many essays that nearly always had to be brief but that pointed out salient characteristics, characteristics not always apparent to others. His judgments of fellow Chileans: Gabriela Mistral, Luis Durand, and Pablo Neruda; of other Latin-Americans: Alfonso Reyes, Borges, and Ricardo Güiraldes; of writers from the United States: Upton Sinclair, Hemingway, and Steinbeck; of Europe: Freud, Marañón, and Havelock Ellis, and his book-length essays on Lao-Tszé, Confucius, and Buddha, written with sympathy, attest to his honesty and magnanimity. Our hope is that the opinions expressed in this brief study have not failed in either of these respects. Although based on opinions of many others, including dozens of Chileans, some of whom knew him intimately, our opinions are those of a North American whose love for Ibero-American men of letters has no limits. They are, nevertheless, those of an outsider. We are emboldened to hope, however, that they may help to round out the total so that all readers may see Juan Marin as he deserves to be seen by present and future generations.

Standing too near a man is almost as conducive to a failure to understand his real character as standing too far from him. Maybe a combination of the near and distant view will help to give a better total idea of what the real Juan Marin was.

J. O. S.

ACKNOWLEDGMENTS

The author of this present study, *Juan Marin—Chilean, the Man and his Writings,* gratefully expresses his gratitude to several organizations and persons: to the American Philosophical Society and the University of Kentucky for grants-in-aid that made it possible for him to spend parts of the summers of 1965, 66, and 68 in Chile to assemble information indispensable in completing his project; to the Biblioteca Nacional of Chile, the library of the Chilean-North American Institute of Santiago, Chile, the Columbus Memorial Library of the Pan American Union, and the Library of Congress for making their collections and other facilities available; to the Pan American Union for permission to quote at length from various items in their program *Homenaje a la Memoria de Juan Marin* and from the essay by Luis Merino Reyes published in the outstanding magazine *Revista Internacional de Bibliografía.*

A minimum of persons that deserve special mention are: Carlos and Esther Vallejo who supplied their inspired translations of some of Dr. Marin's poems; Mr. Frank P. Hebblethwaite for his suggestions concerning *Bibliographies A. and B.;* Professors Charles Ray Beach and Marvin Taylor of Lee College for help with proof reading; Mr. Flavius Lee, Production Manager of the Pathway Press, Mr. Ron Hood, the artist who prepared the cover design for the book, Mr. John D. Golden who had charge of the linotype work and last but not of least importance, Nancy, wife of the undersigned.

J. O. S.

CONTENTS

Prologue

In the evolution of Chilean narrative there is a firm tradition of realism, beginning with Alberto Blest Gana, the powerful interpreter of Chilean society in the Nineteenth Century, through the *criollista* school of Eduardo Barrios, Pedro Prado and Joaquín Edwards Bello, up to the recent generation of neo-realists who search in the rapidly changing environment of Chile for a system of transcendent symbolism.

Juan Marin, poet, short story writer and novelist, is an outstanding figure in that tradition. When he began to write, in the early Twenties, Latin American literature was absorbing the revolutionary changes which hit Europe after the First World War. Mexican, Argentine, Chilean poets followed with enthusiasm the manifestos of Futurism, Surrealism and Creationism. It was a moment of high and wide experimentation. In a subdued manner Gabriela Mistral, Alfonso Reyes, Jorge Borges were in the meantime giving shape to a reaction against the ephemeral brilliance of the *ultraístas,* the Mexican *estridentistas,* and the Chilean *creacionistas.*

At an early stage of his literary career Juan Marin participated in what might be considered a Chilean version of *futurism.* (Cf. *Looping.*) However, his creative impulse soon led him in a different direction. A man of great perspicacity, deeply conscious of social conflicts, Marin could not avoid being impressed by the deteriorated economic conditions of his fellow-countrymen. He then wrote short stories dealing with the life of coal miners in southern Chile. Without preaching or engaging in political propaganda, Juan Marin presented a dramatic, somber, epic image of a society on the verge of a revolutionary crisis.

After the publication of his novels *Viento negro** and *Paralelo 53 sur,* Chilean critics referred to Juan Marin as the successor of Baldomero Lillo, a powerful short-story writer whose descriptions of life in Lota marked the beginning of "proletarian realism"

---

* In this study the titles of Juan Marin's works will usually be given in Spanish, at times, the English title immediately following. In our Bibliography A, *Book Length Publications,* there will be found an English translation for each Spanish title.

in Chilean literature. Juan Marin's novels, however, revealed a link not only with local realism, but with the regionalism of Mariano Azuela, Rómulo Gallegos, and Mariano Latorre. Also, his humanitarian feelings and social criticism connected his work with that of American novelists of the thirties. He was a writer with a deep sense of social commitment and his narrative had a wide impact among Chilean readers.

On the other hand, Juan Marin showed a tendency towards the exotic and the fantastic; he investigated human condition beyond the boundaries of immediate reality. His tales of Magallanes and Aysen perhaps owe more to Melville than to Jack London. This inclination for the mysterious and unexplainable aspects of life in the wilderness gave to his stories in *Cuentos de viento y agua* a supernatural tone.

Having traveled in Egypt, China, and India during the time he served in the diplomatic corps of his country, Juan Marin devoted extensive books to expound the religious and philosophic ideas of those nations. He looked for secret ways to give a transcendent meaning to a reality that appeared violent and agonic to him. He wrote numerous stories with a parapsychological significance that brought him close to writers such as Jorge Luis Borges, Bloy Cásares, and Anderson Imbert, and led away from the old regionalists.

Today, Juan Marin's reputation is firmly established on the basis of three books: *Viento negro,* a novel about coal miners; *Paralelo 53 sur,* an epic tale of life in Magallanes; and *Cuentos de viento y agua* in which Marin masterfully combines his social consciousness and metaphysical visions.

Professor James Swain's book is a well documented introduction to the works of Juan Marin; it will help to make Marin's novels and essays known in the United States. It is to be hoped that Professor Swain's presentation of the most salient facts in Dr. Juan Marin's life, as well as his detailed bibliography and brief analysis of some of his books, will awaken the attention of American readers to the significance of this eminent Chilean writer.

Fernando Alegría, Stanford University

Introduction

This short introduction will serve as a guide which will do three principal things. It will answer the question, "Why Juan Marin?" It will explain the order in which the various phases of the author's works are to be discussed and, finally, it will say something about the methods to be used.

While acting as Visiting Professor of Contemporary American Novel during the sessions of the Escuela de Temporada (Summer School) of the University of Chile in Santiago in 1952, we were pleased to attend lectures by Hugo Goldsack concerning the *Premios Nacionales de Literatura de Chile*. As we visited the many excellent bookstores looking for the works of the *premiados*, others deemed worthy of this honor were mentioned by booksellers. Among these one of the most frequently named was Juan Marin. We were fortunate enough to find: *Viento negro, Cuentos de viento y agua,* and *Naufragio*. A rapid reading of these three aroused our desire to obtain the author's other works. In September of 1955 we were introduced to Dr. Marin by Fernando Alegría in Berkeley, California. A few months later Professor Alegría informed us that the Organization of American States, hereafter abbreviated OAS, had persuaded Dr. Marin to accept the post of Director of Cultural Affairs for the organization. He followed in this post the outstanding Brazilian writer, Erico Veríssimo.

Subsequent visits with Dr. Marin reinforced our determination to collect his entire literary output and to become one of the authorities on the author of *Paralelo 53 sur*. During our conversations with Dr. Marin and while examining his prolific and varied writings, we discovered that he had certain traits that are a matter of great pride to Chileans: patriotism, universalism, intellectual curiosity, industry, and open-mindedness. Reading and rereading his writings convinced us that he had produced notable poetry, prose fiction, medical and religio-philosophical essays, books on civilization and travel, penetrating critical writings, and even some interesting drama.

The fact that Dr. Marin treated the United States with fairness and understanding, pointing out our strong points as well as our weaknesses, may have had some influence on our final decision to dedicate a book-length study to this physician, writer, and diplomat. We should like to point out that he made some very constructive and needed criticism of our country.

When the news of Dr. Marin's untimely death came to us, we wrote a note of condolence to his widow and at the same time proposed that we be allowed to prepare this study. Her answer was in the affirmative. She very generously offered us the use of her complete collection of her late husband's works and her dozens of note-books filled with clippings, a treasure far greater than we had expected. Several grants, three from the American Philosophical Society and one from the University of Kentucky, made it possible for us to spend parts of three summers in Chile.

The study of Juan Marin's writings is presented in the following order:

Biography.

Types of writing: Poetry, Prose Fiction, Philosophies and Civilizations of the Far East, Travel and Interpretation, Medical Writings, and Criticism.

General Conclusions, summation of chapter conclusions—Juan Marin, the Man, and His Writings.

Although the methods used in presenting Dr. Marin's writings will vary somewhat, depending on the type of material, in general we shall avoid extensive quotations. We shall analyze the item; if a quotation from Dr. Marin is indicated, we shall translate or paraphrase briefly in English and, in most cases, quote the original in the *General Notes*. In the case of the poetry, we have thought it important to use more translation, paraphrasing, and quotation than with other writings.

We recognize our debt to many people who have given their help without stint, but we shall mention only a limited number.

Mrs. Marilyn Landers-Terry's excellent study, *The Prose Fiction of Juan Marin,* has been very helpful as we prepared Chapter III, "The Prose Fiction." For some of the translations of Juan Marin's poetry to English we cannot adequately express our gratitude to Carlos and Esther Vallejo. We owe special thanks, also, to Dr. Fernando Alegría, a loyal friend of Dr. and Mrs. Marin and a creative writer widely acclaimed for his critical insight. In addition to advice and suggestions, Dr. Alegría has been kind enough to provide the excellent *Prologue* for this study.

The devoted wife of Juan Marin, Milena Luksic de Marin, to whom we dedicate this modest study, has been indefatigable in helping in more ways than we can acknowledge. We spent many happy mornings in what was her husband's study examining her complete collection of his writings, attended by Milena and her mother. The spirit of Juan Marin seemed to hover near looking down on us from the beautiful painting of the author that faced us as we attempted to express in writing something that would make him understood by future generations. Doña Milena announced to us nearly every day that she had invited to lunch or tea some person who might be able to give a more personal turn to our investigations. Some of these visitors (we cannot, of course, mention more than a very few) were General Alfredo Puga, who was Juan Marin's flight instructor; René Silva Espejo, Director of *El Mercurio de Santiago;* Raúl Silva Castro, a well known critic; Dr. Gustavo Fricke, Dr. Marin's fellow student at the University of Chile's School of Medicine; the writers Luis Oyarzún and Enrique Lafourcade; and Luis Arenas from the Cultural Department of the University of Chile.

Doña Milena was trained as a musician but became one of her husband's best critics. She typed much of his writing and even took many pages down from dictation. As a self-effacing wife she always disclaimed having made any direct contribution to Juan's creative writings, but it is our impression that he often reread aloud many paragraphs to see how they sounded to her. She has a feeling for the poetry of words, both in Spanish and English.

17

As for the present study, Doña Milena collected materials, indicated points of interest, and constantly encouraged us, but the opinions concerning Dr. Marin's literary production are our own. This study does not pretend to be a criticism of Juan Marin's writings. It is, rather, a presentation of the man and his works, especially to English speaking people. Those who read the beautiful language of Cervantes will, we hope, enjoy the rather extensive quotations in our *General Notes* in Spanish.

CHRONOLOGY OF THE MAIN EVENTS IN THE LIFE OF JUAN MARIN

1900, March 23, born in Talca, Chile. (Family lived in Constitución but doctors advised hospitalization of mother in Talca.)

1904-8 Elementary school in Constitución, at that time of only four years.

1908-10 Secondary school in Constitución. At the time the *liceo* (secondary school) of Constitución consisted of two years only.

1910-14 Last four years of *liceo* in Talca. The famous educator-philosopher, Enrique Molina Garmendia, was then the rector (director) of this outstanding secondary school.

1916- First poems appeared in *Jardín profanado*. (See Ch. II.)

1914-21 Medical School of the University of Chile in Santiago. Received degree Doctor of Medicine, October 24, 1921. Dissertation required for the M.D. degree *La tiro-toxicosis y su tratamiento quirúgico (Thyroid Toxicosis and its Surgical Treatment)*.

1918-20 Served as undergraduate assistant in reputed surgical clinic of Dr. Lucas Sierra being chosen because of his superior work during his first years of medical studies.

1921 Appointed Surgical Assistant in Dr. Sierra's well-known clinic.

1922 Promoted to First Assistant in same clinic. During the later years he received a modest stipend, approximately $50.00 per month.

1924-5 Assistant in Barros Luco Polyclinic.

1924-27 Jefe Policlínica de Enfermedades Sociales.

1925-26 Professor of Anatomy in School of Veterinary Medicine, July 1st, 1925 to August 31, 1926.

1925-1928   Médico de Turno de la Asistencia Pública.

1926-27   Professor of Physiology in School of Veterinary Medicine.

1928   Commissioned Lieutenant Surgeon, Naval Air Force.

1929   Transferred to Chilean Navy when Air Force was made separate entity of the Military Services. Attained the rank of Lieutenant Commander (Capitán de Corbeta) before leaving the Navy in 1939.

1929   Attended the first Congress of Military Medicine and Surgery in Valparaíso.

1929   Took part in the first hydroaerial flight to Chiloé.

1929-30   On leave from the Navy Dr. Marin spent two years visiting hospitals and medical schools in Ireland, Scotland, England, and France. (See *Clínicas y maestros en Inglaterra y Francia.*)

1931-2   Stationed in Santiago as Doctor for the Naval Personnel. Director of Free Social Services in Santiago.

1932   Professor of History of Medicine, Medical School of the University of Chile in Santiago. Dr. Marin initiated this professorship. (See pages 7-9 of *Poliedro médico* and Chapter VI of this study.)

1933, January 18, married Milena Luksic.

1933   Named Director of Naval Hospital of Magallanes (Punta Arenas) where he remained until March, 1935.

1933   Chief of the Miraflores Hospital in Magallanes while still in charge of the Naval Medical Services.

1935-7   To comply with a naval ruling, he spent two years aboard the naval vessel *Almirante Latorre.* (It was during these years that he finished the novel *Paralelo 53 sur,* considered by many as his masterpiece.)

1936   Visited Naval and Military hospitals in Washington, D. C. and Philadelphia.

1937-39   Assigned to the School of Communications of the Navy, Las Salinas, Viña del Mar, where he remained until he entered the Diplomatic Corps. Note: During these years Dr. Marin was very active in a number of medical societies and services. It is interesting to note how much of his time he dedicated to literary activities: editor of *Vida médica,* founder of *Revista chilena de pediatría,* collaborator to *Medicina moderna, Boletín médico, Letras,* etc.

1938   Elected President of the Medical Society of Valparaíso.

1938   Director of the Department of Culture of the city of Viña del Mar.

1939   Named by President Aguirre Cerda as Chargé d'Affaires and Consul General to China where he remained until September, 1943 when he was repatriated. (The Japanese had invaded Shanghai and in January, 1943 closed the Chilean diplomatic offices.)

1944-6   Planned to go to the Chinese capital, Chungking, by flying "over the hump" but while awaiting transportation in Washington, there arose a need for his services in the republic of El Salvador.

1946   Sent again to China as Chargé d'Affaires to reopen Chilean legation.

1947   Sent to Manila as Chile's special envoy to attend the celebrations of Independence Day of the Philippines.

1947-49   Sent to Egypt as Chargé d'Affaires. At the same time he acted as Chargé d'Affaires for Chile in Syria and Lebanon.

1949-52   Chargé d'Affaires in India.

1952   President Ibáñez accepted Dr. Marin's automatic resignation from his diplomatic post; he returned to Chile at the end of December via Paris, London, Spain, and the United States, arriving in Chile in March 1953.

1953-63   Contributing Editor of *El Mercurio.* Published articles in nearly all the newspapers and magazines of Spanish America plus many in the U.S.A. (*La opinión,* Los Angeles; *La semana,* Guayaquil; *Diario latino,* San Salvador; *La nueva democracia,* New York; etc.)

1953-55 Lectured at various branches of the University of Chile.

1954 Elected president of the Writers Society of Chile.

1954 Accepted appointment as Sub-Director of the Chilean-Northamerican Institute, Santiago.

1954 Was invited by the government of Egypt as representative of *El Mercurio* to help celebrate 1st anniversary of Egypt's independence.

1956 Was invited by the Department of State of the U.S.A. to make an official visit to our country. (Visited the sessions of the Instituto Internacional de Literatura Iberoamericana in Berkeley.)

1956 Accepted appointment as Director of Cultural Affairs of the OAS (Pan American Union) in Washington, D. C., following another distinguished novelist, Erico Veríssimo. Took possession of the office in October, 1956. Attended several international conferences: Punto del Este, Unesco in Paris, etc.

1961, March Received the David Prize awarded by the International Renaissance Society in recognition of work in office of Director of Cultural Relations for the OAS.

1962 Named director of the International Summer School in Valparaíso, sponsored by several universities of Chile, the OAS, and the Department of State of the USA.

1963, Feb. 10 Died in his sleep in Valparaíso.

1963, Feb. 12 Buried with military honors in Santiago.

1963, March 20 A special meeting was held in the Hall of the Americas of the Pan American Union, Washington, D. C. to honor the memory of Dr. Marin.

Posthumous honors:

A postgraduate scholarship in Engineering, *The Juan Marin Scholarship,* was established in the Federico Santa María Technical University of Santiago.

In Guayaquil, Ecuador an educational foundation, *The Juan Marin Educational Center,* has been established.

CHAPTER I

Biography

Because a man's life takes on deeper meaning when framed by the influences that mold his character, it will be well to examine them. These influences may be listed as: racial background, environment, and epoch—the famous *race, milieu et moment*. We accept the proposition that no one, not even the most individualistic of writers, can isolate himself from his surroundings. This does not mean that Juan Marin resigned himself to things as they existed. Far from it! He always reacted, positively or negatively but never violently, as he developed his personal social and literary philosophy.

In so far as *race* is concerned, suffice it to say that Juan Marin was a Chilean who, having been brought up in a semi-isolated small city, Constitución, was spared foreign influences during his earlier years. His broader nationalism and his cosmopolitanism were developed after his tenth year, first in the provincial capital, Talca, where he finished his secondary schooling, next in Santiago, a city that when he began his medical studies at the age of fourteen was becoming international, and eventually in Europe, 1929-31, when he was undergoing and analyzing the experiences reported in *Clínicas y maestros en Inglaterra y Francia*. But in spite of these broadening experiences, he remained Chilean through and through to the end of his life.

Milieu (environment), however, was of great importance as Juan Marin's character was developing. One can safely say that Chile is one of the most advanced of the Spanish American countries, educationally, culturally and spiritually. As early as the time of Ercilla, the writer (especially the poet) was held in high

23

esteem. But if we skip over a fairly long period of time we discover that soon after her independence from Spain, near the midcentury, the importance of the writer and of literature was accentuated by the reorganization of the University of Chile under the direction of Andrés Bello, a distinguished grammarian and poet. The several visits and periods of residence in Chile of another great intellectual, Domingo Faustino Sarmiento, were not lacking in influence on the cultural life of the republic.

It must not be forgotten, however, that if the way had not been prepared by native Chileans, these two great educational philosophers would not have accomplished what they did. Many very important Chilean and foreign educators, whose names we shall not list, continued the work already begun, leading directly into what is often called the *Generation of 1920*.[1] Many critics and historians of Chilean letters insist on denying the existence of this *Generation of 1920;* we, however, shall accept its existence as legitimate and place Dr. Marin among its leading writers.

Because of her geography, Chile has always been a seafaring nation. Many writers, like Juan Marin, have chosen to write about the sea. Among others that one might well mention are: Augusto d'Halmar, Salvador Reyes, Benjamín Subercaseaux, and Francisco Coloane.[2] In her few wars, for Chile has been on the whole a peace-loving nation, her navy has been her salvation. But the sea is always present in the thoughts of the typical Chilean; her ships are seen in all the ports of the world. The sailor in Chile is universally admired and respected. In spite of the large number of citizens of foreign parentage, Chile is racially unified.

One of the most popular among contemporary writers, Benjamín Subercaseaux, produced a book with the title, *Chile, o una loca geografía (Chile or an Absurd Geography)*. Chile may well have an absurd, but at the same time an interesting, geography: the highest of the Andes, the deepest of the Pacific deeps just off the Chilean coast (often blamed for the many earthquakes and tremors), beautiful inland lakes, lands with rainfall a forgotten phenomenon and others with more than one hundred fifty inches per year, to mention only a few geographical extremes. From the arid, treeless plains of the north, through the temperate and agriculturally rich central region, on past the rain drenched, heavily forested zone between Concepción and Puerto Montt, through the winding inner passages to the Straits of Magellan, political, intellectual, and military leaders constantly converge on Santiago, the cultural center of Chile. From this beautiful capital one can be in the foot-hills of the Andes in an hour or on one of the attractive beaches of the Pacific in the same period of time.

Insofar as *moment* or time is concerned, the *Generation of 1920* was greatly influenced by the naval and military victories of the War of the Pacific.* The University of Chile in Santiago had become, under Andrés Bello and others, an outstanding one in the New World by bringing in as many as two thousand foreign students per year to study under the native and foreign professors. Many of the latter were the most highly trained that Europe had to offer. Even from the United States hundreds of students and young professors came to attend the famed *Escuela de Temporada* (Summer Session). In return many of the most promising graduates from the universities of Chile come to the United States to lend us their educational and cultural leadership—at the same time continuing their artistic activities in their homeland with a slightly modified perspective.[3]

Many of the writers who began their production with the *Generation of 1920* and who virtually completed their work by 1950 show, some more others less, the influence of this period of relative intellectual, economic, and political stability. Some of the recent economic and social reforms designed to redistribute natural resources, including land, and to provide more equal opportunities to the proletariat affected the *Generation of 1920* very little.

Fortunately for Chile, and the world of letters at large, the

* Although the dates of the War of the Pacific are usually given as 1879-1884, the full effects of the long conflict were not felt until the treaty of 1904 was signed.

desire to participate in creative literature has continued. To encourage artistic endeavor, the national government has established, among other awards, the *Premio Nacional de Literatura*[4] (National Literary Prize).

For a country with a population of slightly more than eight millions (census of 1952), Chile has a large number of excellent publishing houses, some as modern in equipment as the best in Europe or North America. Literary magazines and literary supplements in the newspapers are further proof of the almost universal respect and love for *belles lettres* in Chile.[5]

First Period (1900-1914)

The first period in the life of Dr. Marin extends from his birth through secondary school. In *Orestes y yo (Orestes and I)* there are certain pages that might be construed to be slightly autobiographical, but knowing how easy it is to be misled by reading into an author's writings hints of his biography, we shall omit direct quotations from that most interesting novel. Juan Marin was born on March 23, 1900[6] in Talca, Chile. The family was still living in Constitución; following the advice of her doctor, however, Juan Marin's mother went to Talca, some 75 miles away, for his birth. When Urbano Marin, Juan's older brother, prepared to enter school in 1904, Juan, three years his junior, insisted that he be allowed to attend also. The fact that Juan Marin began school so early gave rise to a mistake in his birth date. We have seen a copy of his birth certificate and also his passport; both give the aforementioned date.[7] Much to the surprise of his parents and teachers, Juan did excellent work. Urbano and Juan attended the secondary school in Constitución for the two years offered then in that city. This meant that in 1910 when Juan was only ten years of age the two boys had to transfer to the Liceo de Talca to continue their schooling. Urbano was destined for the legal profession while Juan and a younger brother were to prepare themselves to be physicians.

When the two Marin boys came to enroll in the Liceo de Talca

(The Talca secondary school), Don Enrique Molina[8], the Rector, accepted Urbano readily enough but said to Juan, "You are too young to go into the third year; you will have to start in the first." But Juan, usually quite docile, insisted on his rights, saying, "I have finished two years at Constitución with excellent grades; I see no reason to repeat two years here!" Don Enrique Molina agreed to allow Juan to enter the third year on trial, and nothing more was said about his being too young. Juan was, according to those who remember him, small for his age at that time. He continued to grow until at twenty he was over six feet tall, though he remained slender for some years.

At that time, the secondary school in Talca was dominated by the clergy. More attention was given to promoting conformity than in awakening intellectual curiosity in the students. Don Enrique, whose main interests were in philosophy, would not accept the pernicious influence of obscurantism. Pressure was brought to bear and for some time it appeared that a new Rector would be named. But Don Enrique, with the support of other persons who wanted to have a first rate secondary school in Talca, was able to carry out his reforms. He had as Vice-Rector, Alejandro Venegas, another inspiring teacher.

The combination of the liberalism of Juan's father and the influence of his professors' philosophic thought led the young student to a humanism that rose above any particular religious tendencies; many of his writings show his keen interest in the history of religion. Not being strong physically and two years younger than most of the boys in his class, he gave much of his spare time to reading under the guidance of his teachers. Although we have no exact list of what he read, we do know from reliable sources that his craving for knowledge took him deeply into the principal works of European (including the ancient Greeks), American, and Latin-American philosophers, poets, and dramatists. Of these wide readings we shall mention only a few— European: Shakespeare, Cervantes, Rousseau, Zola, Balzac, Dostoevsky, Tolstoy, Victor Hugo, Rimbaud, Baudelaire, Dante,

27

Wilde, Byron, and Juan Ramón Jiménez; Latin American: Rubén Darío, Amado Nervo, and Herrera y Reissig; North American: Whitman, Poe, Thoreau, Emerson, John Dewey, and William James. Many other writers are mentioned and quoted in the writings of Juan Marin but the above are significant.

In the Liceo of Talca by rare coincidence a group of remarkably gifted young men came together and developed an active literary life in addition to their school studies. Alejandro Venegas, Professor of Spanish, encouraged their first works in the field of literature. He inaugurated a regular program, *Charlas literarias (Literary Talks)*, which became very well known in Talca and news of it even reached Santiago. This regional literary movement had great importance in the future development of Chilean *belles lettres*. Many of the teachers and students involved in it later attained distinguished positions in the cultural life of the country.

Second Period (1914-1928)

It is interesting to note that Juan Marin came to Santiago to matriculate in the Medical School when he was just fourteen years of age. Had his record in the Liceo not been nearly perfect, his age would have made it impossible for him to begin his medical studies so early.

This second period in the life of our author is often passed over, allowing the casual reader to believe that nothing of importance was happening to the future writer. But the years from ages 14 to 28 in any man's life are always important. We have seen dozens of articles written at this time by Juan Marin, many in magazines published by his contemporaries. One must keep in mind the fact that the medical student of Latin America is not isolated from cultural activities. Although we cannot accept anyone's creative writings as biography, there is always some connection, more or less indicative of real life happenings, in even the most imaginative literature. In one of the stories dealing with student life, "El 'Curco' Meléndez,"[9] we are led to believe that along with other medical students the studious Juan Marin had his moments of relaxation and took part in extracurricular activities. Two of the poems in *Looping* are dedicated to Juan Marin's friends, probably fellow students. "Bataclán" has the dedicatory salutation "A los alegres amigos de Catedral 1165" (To the happy friends of Cathedral 1165)[10] and another one from the same collection "Josephine Baker"[10a] is dedicated "A los artistas del cenáculo de Sierra Bella 1266" (To the artists of the Sierra Bella Literary Club).

One evening we were returning from the National Library where they had just made for us a micro-film of *Looping*. On one of the busiest streets of Santiago a new automobile was being raffled off "to provide travel grants to two outstanding medical students who would be sent to Europe." After investing five *escudos* in the education of said students, we struck up a conversation with one of the bright-eyed *médicos*. He noted immediately that Spanish was not my native language and asked me in reasonably good English, "Are you American?" Eventually we got around to talking about Juan Marin.

"Oh, yes," he said, evidently quite proud to realize that he could give me some information about the author of *Paralelo*. . . . "He was once the professor of The History of Medicine in our medical school. We all read his *Clínicas y maestros en Inglaterra y Francia*."

Having talked briefly with Luis Durand, author of *Fronteras,* one of the best regional novels to come out of Chile, we were interested to read in his criticism of Juan Marin's first novel *Margarita* . . . a reference to the young doctor's activities in Santiago:

> We hardly know the author of the book, *Margarita*. . . .
> Once or twice we have talked with him briefly. . . . At
> one time or another we remember having read his book
> reviews; then we saw him in a meeting of the Writers
> Society . . . and once while eating in one of the downtown
> restaurants we heard him on the radio giving a lecture
> having to do with his profession. . . .[11]

One could cite many places in our author's creative writings that give us deeper insight into his multiple activities during the years discussed in this period of his life, but we feel that we need not belabor the point. As he grew older he began to be more selective but he always was involved in numerous meaningful movements.

In spite of other interests that attracted Juan Marin, the medical student, he did not neglect attendance at lectures or laboratories of the excellent School of Medicine of the University of Chile. It is our impression, received from many long conversations with Chilean medical school professors, that the level of medical education in the School of Medicine of the University of Chile in Santiago had reached a high plane.

Juan Marin plunged into his studies with such enthusiasm and hard work that he soon came to the notice of his professors. These professors recommended him to Dr. Lucas Sierra, an outstanding surgeon and teacher, who invited him to become one of the undergraduate assistants in his famous surgical clinic. An assistantship in Dr. Sierra's clinic brought many honors and a number of special advantages. At a time when very few universities offered residencies leading to specialization, such clinics allowed a small number of medical students to emphasize a more limited field, in this case surgery. After he had ended his basic training, Juan Marin was induced to continue as Chief Assistant to Dr. Lucas Sierra.

A very promising career was open to our young Doctor Marin. His formal training finished and his dissertation, *La tiro-toxicosis y su tratamiento quirúgico,*[12] published, he explored many other fields of medical service in addition to continuing his work in the Lucas Sierra Clinic. Nor did he neglect his interest in critical and creative writing! He continued to contribute to many newspapers and magazines. Many of his experiences, both before and after receiving his M.D. degree, enter into his later creative writings. The struggle between the writer and the practicing physician had already begun.

A typical young doctor in Santiago often carries on several assignments simultaneously. Some held by Dr. Marin were: Chief of the Clinical Services of the Workers' Accident Insurance Society in 1925 and Physician in attendance at the Asistencia Pública in 1926-1927-1928. Also he was usually editor of some magazine. He entered into all of these fields of endeavor with his usual enthusiasm and determination to excel.

Third Period (1928-1939)

Then the question often arises, "Why did a young M.D., who had the support of his professors (including the noted surgeon Lucas Sierra), many loyal friends, influential relatives, and an enviable record in his medical studies, decide to enter the military establishment?" Dr. Marin often mentions writers and diplomats who had faced similar decisions: Duhamel, Maughan, etc. He realized, of course, that a surgeon in private practice could aspire to an income many times that of an officer in the air force or navy.

His first military assignment was in the Chilean Naval Air Force. Any new undertaking was a challenge to Juan Marin! As a medical officer he had no obligation to learn how to fly, how to pilot a plane, but he felt that such an accomplishment would help him understand the problems faced by the men whose mental and physical health he would have to supervise; he would be more effective if his knowledge of flying were more than superficial. The role that planes and aviation had in his writings cannot be overemphasized. Its importance can be readily observed in his first book of poems, *Looping* (1929), in his best collection of short stories, *Alas sobre el mar (Wings Over the Sea)*, and in his novel, *Un avión volaba* (1935) *(A Plane Was Flying)*, as well as in many of his other productions of creative fiction. One of his best poems in *Looping* gives its name to the whole volume. In the same collection the poem "Superavión"[13] also shows the place that aviation had in his heart. The first poem in *Looping* "Spin"[14] beginning "Canción . . . Oh . . . Canción" and dedicated to his flight instructor Alfredo Puga (later General Puga) is an additional indication of Juan Marin's love for planes and flying.

While serving on the battleship *Almirante Latorre,* which was en route to England, Dr. Marin was released from active duty to visit famous doctors and medical schools in Great Britain and France. Fortunately he had continued his interest in English and French so that it was possible for him to make excellent use of his time in Europe. His very informative book, *Clínicas y maestros en Inglaterra y Francia* (1931), gives an interesting and detailed report on his experiences and observations in Europe. The notes gathered during this period became a part of his lectures delivered while he was professor of the History of Medicine at the University of Chile Medical School in 1932. *(See Poliedro médico.)* We understand that the remaining lectures will soon be published. They deserve publication for besides the information they contain one notices evidences of his developing literary style. If we accept as a sample of the care with which Dr. Marin prepared his lectures, one with the title of "Hipócrates y el hipocratismo" (Hippocrates and Hippocratism),[15] we may well expect a very valuable contribution to the history of medicine.

But before leaving Chile for Europe, Marin had delivered to a publisher his first book of verse, *Looping.* Many of the poems of this collection had previously appeared in *PROA* (Buenos Aires) and other magazines and had received some favorable reviews but on the whole they did not arouse the attention they merited. These poems show inspiration and intense poetic feeling. More will be said about *Looping* in a later chapter.

In October of 1931 Dr. Marin was back in Chile. As a naval doctor he could have dedicated part of his time to writing, but there were many other things to do, especially for a conscientious young medic who had recently visited some of the best hospitals and medical schools of Europe. Dr. Marin carried on, besides his duties to the naval personnel, dozens of civilian activities. The list of his positions and extra-medical activities is almost unbelievable. His interests included pediatrics, social diseases, maternal assistance, and birth control as well as a continuing dedication to his first love, surgery. He was waging a hopeless fight against his desire to write by accepting all manner of new assignments in the broad field of medicine.

In 1935, to meet a requirement that all naval officers must serve some time aboard one of the commissioned ships, he was appointed fleet surgeon on the *Almirante Latorre.* The two years afloat were of almost unalloyed pleasure. Dr. Marin throughout his entire life was a lover of the sea; while on the *Almirante Latorre* his medical services were limited to looking after the crew, which meant that he had time to continue writings already begun and to start others that he would complete later. In spite of the multiplicity of his activities in the navy in 1928-1939, the list of his publications during these years is quite impressive.[16]

Juan Marin, however, was beginning to feel the need of new and more cosmopolitan experiences. His two years in Europe had reawakened in him a compelling desire to see distant places— to become really international in his writings. It is not strange, therefore, that he accepted quite willingly an appointment in the Chilean diplomatic service. Such an appointment is not unusual, for Chile has often rewarded her men of letters with diplomatic assignments and while the salaries paid to consular and diplomatic personnel are modest, there are other incentives in the Foreign Service. In June 1939 President Pedro Aguirre Cerda appointed doctor Juan Marin as Chargé d'Affaires and Consul General of Chile in China. These were years of intense activities on the part of Dr. Marin and his gifted wife, Doña Milena.

It is well to say something here about Doña Milena. She was studying piano in Santiago, where her family lived. Though she was quite young, her teachers felt that with her talents and enthusiasm she was meant to become an outstanding pianist. When she met Juan Marin, he was already a surgeon of high standing and had also become well known for some of his writings. They were married on January 18, 1933.

After their marriage, Milena immediately began to devote all

33

her energies to helping her husband with his varied interests. For that reason she could not give much time to her piano though she continued for a while with her studies. It is said that during the first years of her husband's diplomatic career Milena would comply with requests of their friends to perform on the piano. But she put the activities of her husband first and was, we are sure, a great help to him in an infinite number of ways, even assisting him in operations when these took place in remote hospitals where professional nurses were not available. Doña Milena had become quite conversant with the many problems related to the preparation of drafts for books to be printed: proof reading, and other details in connection with publications. Her knowledge and use of English, oral and written, are excellent. This has been quite valuable for the Marins constantly consulted authoritative books in English.

Fourth Period (1939-1952)

The Fourth Period in the life of Dr. Marin was very important and filled with adventures, even physical hardships and dangers. At the same time he did not give up writing. If anything, he wrote even more, not in the number of titles but in the length of his books, some of which contained more than three hundred closely printed pages.[17] As mentioned before, the first diplomatic assignment of the Marins was China, at that time partly occupied by the Japanese armies.

The years in China were very busy ones, for Dr. Marin felt that one ought to have more than a superficial knowledge of the culture, philosophies, and civilization of the countries to which he was appointed. Having found an excellent library of books on China, mostly in English and French, our novelist spent many hours documenting himself on his new country. This unlimited intellectual curiosity is shown in his books: *El emperador Kwang-Hsü*) (1941), *China (China)* (1944),[18] *El alma de China (The Soul of China)* (1945), *Mesa de mah-jong (The Mah-jong Table)* (1945), and *Muerte en Shanghai (Death in Shanghai)* (1953). These publications will be discussed at length later.

The first few months of the occupation of Shanghai by the Japanese army were rewarding ones to the Marins in spite of the frustrations caused by their status as quasi-prisoners. Not being able to travel over the rest of China and with his every movement watched by the invaders, Dr. Marin continued his study of the country and completed additional writings. The information and atmosphere for *Muerte en Shanghai* were being accumulated although the novel was not published until 1953. When a state of war was declared between Japan and the United States, Dr. Marin offered the services of the Chilean diplomatic and consular corps for the protection of American interests. Eventually Chile was forced to sever diplomatic relations with Japan and the quisling Chinese government; the Marins were repatriated by the Swedish neutral ship *The Gripsholm*. An interesting and flattering reference to Dr. Marin's services to the American government was read into the *Congressional Record* by Senator Wayne Morse:

> Mr. Morse: Mr. President, Mr. Richard Butrick, a retired
> Foreign Service officer residing in the District of Columbia,
> has informed me of the death of Dr. Juan Marin.[19]
> (See Note 30 for a complete transcription of this speech
> by Senator Morse.)

We cannot insist too much on Dr. Marin's understanding of and love for the real pre-communist China. He would have been quite happy to spend the rest of his life as Chile's representative in the *Land of the Dragon*. His contributions as a diplomat in Egypt, El Salvador, and India were outstanding but there seems to run through Dr. Marin's later life a nostalgia for his beloved China. Such writings as *Mesa de mah-Jong*, "El derrumbe del cielo," and *El emperador Kwang-Hsü* indicate his special interest in the Chinese.

Soon after the Marins arrived back in Chile, the Chinese established a new capital in Chungking. In the meantime President Aguirre Cerda had died and his successor, Juan Antonio Ríos, asked Juan Marin to return to his diplomatic duties by flying "over the hump." At this time certain rumors of political unrest in El Salvador made it necessary for Chile to send an experienced, top-flight diplomat to represent the country there. Although Dr. Marin's chief concern was China, he accepted the post in San Salvador with the understanding that it was a temporary assignment and that when affairs became more normal he would be able to resume his duties in the Orient.

So the Marins moved to San Salvador early in 1944 where they remained until the spring of 1946, two very fruitful years. During a part of this time one of the few revolutions that have taken place in that enlightened republic gave Dr. Marin a chance to use his extraordinary diplomatic abilities. The Marins were received immediately with open arms in the capital city where they already knew many people.

During our short sojourn in San Salvador it was our good fortune to talk at length with several people with whom the Marins were closely related. One of these, at whose home we spent a very pleasant evening (Dr. Hugo Lindo, also a writer of repute), had lived for some time in Chile and was able to see that the newcomers were rapidly introduced to other prominent people of the city. The famous periodical, *El diario latino*[20], used many of the articles that Dr. Marin was constantly writing. The February 29, 1945 edition of this newspaper was dedicated to Dr. Marin and published generous selections from: *Looping, Lao-Tszé, El Tibet misterioso, Viento negro, Paralelo 53 sur,* etc. A most interesting sketch first published in Santiago and reprinted in San Salvador, "El lago de Costepeque de El Salvador," shows Dr. Marin's constant preoccupation with increasing his knowledge of the country in which he happened to be located. Even though he realized that his appointment to El Salvador was only temporary, he had the intellectual curiosity to want to discover and discuss the salient features of this interesting republic.

With the withdrawal of the Japanese forces from China, the Chinese Government started preparations to return to Nanking. Dr. Marin was asked to go back to China to reopen the Chilean

Legation; the very dangerous trip was made before travel was safe in the Pacific. He recounts the story of this trip in "Viaje en el *Hurricane*."[21] Besides the works mentioned before, our novelist turned out dozens of articles, short-stories, and monographs on China showing in them much more than a superficial knowledge of Chinese philosophy, art, music, politics, and literature.

Two very interesting diplomatic missions came during this period to the Marins. Dr. Marin was a delegate to the ceremony organized in Manila to celebrate Independence Day of the Islands, July 4, 1946. Later, having been asked to represent Chile in Egypt, the Marins (on their journey to the land of the Nile) visited India in August 1947 to attend the independence ceremonies there. Dr. Juan Marin and his wife, now real world travelers, reached Egypt in September of 1947. While stationed in Egypt, he was also Chargé d'Affaires for Syria and Lebanon.

As they had done in China and were to do again in India, the Marins began immediately to get acquainted with their new country. The reports of their travels in Egypt are recorded in the very interesting book, *El Egipto de los faraones (Egypt of the Pharaohs)*, a cooperative work for which Doña Milena took nearly all the pictures. This publication has merited several printings and the *Premio Atenea* (1954) from the University of Concepción, Chile as the best book published during the year.

In March 1949, after negotiating with the Indian Ambassador in Egypt the establishment of diplomatic relations between Chile and India, Dr. Marin was appointed Chargé d'Affaires to that country. He had the honor of opening the first Chilean Legation in New Delhi.

Again the Marins began systematically to gain personal knowledge of their new country, making trips that were difficult, dangerous, and tiresome. The very sympathetic book on India, *La India eterna (Eternal India)*, resulted also from the cooperation of Juan Marin and his wife, Doña Milena.

But all diplomatic appointments are subject to political caprices. The presidential elections of 1952 had given a plurality to Don

37

Carlos Ibáñez; the Chilean congress declared him duly elected. Automatically all persons holding appointive positions in the diplomatic services tendered their resignations. Along with many others, Dr. Marin's resignation was accepted. Unfortunately, many republics lose the services of experienced and skilful ambassadors, as well as top flight consular officers, when a new political party comes to power. After outstanding performance of duties in four countries: China, El Salvador, Egypt, and India, in addition to other casual missions on special occasions, the Marins were relieved of their diplomatic assignment.

Fifth Period (1952-1956)

We have mentioned previously that Dr. Marin realized the importance of discipline, of following the rules, even when he had every reason to feel that decisions were not for the best. He had probably expected to continue as a member of the diplomatic corps for life, but he immediately began formulating new plans, feeling that there was somewhere a need for him in the service of his country.

The Marins returned to Chile via England, France, Italy, Spain, and the United States. Dr. Marin left in Spain for publication a novel in which he allowed his imagination to create a thrilling story of the Japanese occupation, a novel of international political intrigue.[22] Material for many other novels and short stories was, without doubt, in his mind or in outline form awaiting his leisure to finish preparing it for publication.

It was at this time that Dr. Marin started writing his book on Egypt, *El Egipto de los faraones (Egypt of the Pharaohs)*. He was appointed to the editorial staff of *El Mercurio,* one of the most important newspapers printed in Spanish America; his articles were reprinted in other newspapers and magazines in Chile and abroad. He was invited to lecture in nearly all of the branches of the University of Chile. He was elected President of the Chilean-Arab Institute, Director of the Instituto Helénico, and to membership in other bi-national institutes.

Dr. Marin was a very loyal Chilean and at the same time a citizen of the world. His interest in and sympathy for the United States and North Americans were criticized by a few who had learned that the easiest way to gain friends with a certain number of Spanish Americans is to point out our weaknesses. He could, of course, see things in North American politics, philosophy, and civilization not one hundred percent acceptable to him, and he did what he could constructively to help make North Americans see ways in which to improve their world image.

He had given without stint of his time and energies to assist in the work being attempted by the Chilean-North American Institute of Santiago, and finally he accepted a position as Sub-Director of the Institute; he put to good use his wide experiences with such enterprises. One finds in the archives of this institute many evidences of his valuable contributions. The staff still recalls his almost unlimited energy and his cheerful acceptance of suggestions for plans to make more effective the Institute's program.

In April of 1954 he was elected President of the Chilean Writers Society and in July the Egyptian government invited journalists from various countries to attend the celebration of the first anniversary of the founding of the republic in "the land of the Pharaohs." Dr. Marin was designated the delegate from the *Mercurio de Santiago.*

Sixth Period (1956-1963)

In 1955 the Northamerican Department of State invited Dr. Marin to make an official visit to the United States. He gave a number of lectures at various universities. While in California he attended the sessions of the International Institute of Ibero-american Literature[23] scheduled for late August and early September of 1955, in Berkeley. Two fellow Chileans, Dr. Arturo Torres Rioseco and Dr. Fernando Alegría, were very active in organizing the 1955 sessions, the former being President of the Institute for the years 1953-1955. At this meeting we met Dr.

Marin for the first time. Dr. Alegría,[24] who besides being a well known critic is a novelist of growing fame, made the presentations. Our first impressions, published in 1964, are as follows:

> If my memory does not fail me, it was during the last days of August of 1955, in Berkeley, California, that the brilliant young professor and novelist, Dr. Fernando Alegría, also a Chilean, introduced me to Dr. Marin, saying:
>
> "When Professor Swain was in Chile from December 1951 to July 1952, he did not have the pleasure of meeting you. You were still in India."
>
> As I took the proffered hand, I noted that Dr. Marin was tall and athletic. His glance was steady and penetrating but at the same time friendly. He put me entirely at my ease. Without being effusive or in any sense a 'back-slapper', he seemed to radiate a warmth that invited sincerity from the very first words. His voice was deep but well modulated. Being a Chilean with a profound love for his country, he showed great appreciation when I mentioned writers and professors that I had met during my nearly eight months in Chile. Especially was he glad to discover that I had known fairly well Enrique Molina, Luis Durand, Mariano Latorre, González Vera, and Eduardo Barrios. When I confessed that I had not read his novel *Paralelo 53 sur*, he excused himself and returned a few minutes later with a copy autographed as follows: *"Al profesor James O. Swain, verdadero amigo de todo lo chileno"* (To Professor James O. Swain, true friend of everything that is Chilean).[25]

Needless to say, this autographed copy of *Paralelo 53 sur* is one of our most prized possessions. During the four days of the sessions of the I.I.L.I., it was our good fortune to converse with Dr. Marin several times.

A short time later we learned that Dr. Marin had been appointed to the position of Director of Cultural Affairs of the Organization of American States (OAS). This assignment carries only a modest salary when one realizes its importance. People like the Marins who enjoyed entertaining their many friends had to budget carefully. Doña Milena, in addition to being a very charming hostess, learned to shop wisely and even to prepare with her own hands many exotic dishes. An invitation to the Marin home was always coveted.

It was our duty as Executive Secretary of *Sigma Delta Pi,* the National Spanish Honor Society, to set up the triennial meeting in Washington, D. C., for December 1956. We were fortunate enough to have Dr. José Mora, General Secretary of the OAS, accept the invitation to be the principal orator at our official banquet. On a trip to Washington to make final arrangements, we stopped in to talk for a moment with Dr. Mora. He suggested that I visit Dr. Marin in his office in another building.

After introducing me to his staff, he explained what he had accomplished and talked about his plans to extend the services of his department. As he had formerly done on accepting new positions in China, India, Egypt, and El Salvador, he was making a scientific and conscientious evaluation of the possibilities of his new office. The main difficulty, of course, was the matter of deciding which activity would have precedence. He listened attentively to our suggestions. One of these was that he and his wife, Milena, make a tour of the Southeastern States. He showed great interest in a report I made of a visit of his predecessor as cultural officer of the OEA, Dr. Erico Veríssimo, and became quite excited as I pointed out on a map places to be visited. Doubtlessly Dr. Marin had given high priority to such a trip, for he enjoyed travel and was very eager to see the homeland of Thomas Wolfe, Erskine Caldwell, William Faulkner, and others whose novels he had read. Veríssimo had lectured in English, Spanish, and Portuguese in several university centers. Men with such excellent use of English and extraordinarily wide reading as these two possessed do much to help us realize what important work they are doing for inter-cultural relations. These are only two of the many outstanding men of high cultural attainment that have graced the office of Director of Cultural Relations for the OAS.

Our first impression on seeing Dr. and Mrs. Juan Marin together was, "What a striking couple!" Dr. Marin was tall, had a bronzed complexion, stood slightly over six feet, and always had a dignified but pleasant expression. Doña Milena, a blonde, is tall for a woman. She was the cynosure of all eyes but she seemed to have a natural desire to transfer the attention that naturally came her way to Dr. Marin. He, in his turn, always included Doña Milena in conversations directed to him.

After this first meeting, we were in the company of the Marins several times: at Modern Language meetings in New York, Washington, and Chicago, and at meetings of the International Institute of Iberoamerican Literature. Having spent some time in Chile, maybe we took more interest in the Director of Cultural Affairs than might otherwise have been the case. It gave us great pleasure to see how soon the Marins made friends both in Washington and at the international meetings. Muna Lee (whom they had met previously in Chile), Dr. and Mrs. Francisco Aguilera in Washington, Francisco Monterde in Mexico, Luis Muñoz Marin and Dr. José Balseiro of Puerto Rico are only a few who were of great help in introducing the Marins to other persons of accomplishments and culture.

We have mentioned several times the intellectual curiosity that was one of the essential traits of Dr. Juan Marin's personality. Had he lived a few years longer he would have written a book about our country, something similar to *Mesa de mah-jong* or *La India eterna*.[26] His knowledge was not superficial nor based entirely on his wide readings. He was always looking for the *"Soul of the United States."* We recall having had occasion to remark, during one of our many conversations, about the materialism of our country. His answer was something like this: "There are short-comings and greatnesses in your country; we must not forget your great writers, musicians, and other artists."

Juan Marin, like many other persons of excellent health, had little cause to suspect an early death; he had probably hoped to continue with his work at the OAS until some of his projects and programs were implemented. Many times, however, he talked of returning to his country to work on books planned that he needed time to finish. He even discussed with Doña Milena preparing an autobiography including their experiences in the different countries where they had lived. He realized that his many duties as cultural officer for the OAS did not leave him the time needed for extensive creative writing.

But Dr. Marin seemed to have an irrepressible compulsion to write. He tried in vain to satisfy this all-consuming desire by sending back to Santiago hundreds of articles on a wide variety of subjects. His interest in aviation and in medicine had continued unabated so that it is not surprising that he dealt with these. But his best articles were concerned with fiction writers, such as Hemingway, Upton Sinclair, Faulkner, and Steinbeck. A book containing his criticism of American Literature will, we are sure, eventually be published.[27]

Besides the occasional visits with Dr. Marin in his office in the new wing of the Pan American Building, visits that acquainted us with the progress already made and his plans for new activities, we were constantly advised by his colleagues of his excellent work and cheerful disposition. Once, however, we found Dr. Marin somewhat pessimistic; he had fallen while walking through the snowy streets of Washington, D. C. and broken his right arm. Although he had continued to carry on his work as usual, he could not make all the personal appearances and trips he had planned. Usually he had to do a lot of traveling to the different countries of the Americas and to meetings at various universities in the United States. He had just been asked to organize and direct an intensive Inter-American summer session in Valparaíso, Chile during the month of January 1963 and would have to go to Chile to make final arrangements. Previous to this trip he and his wife expected to attend the General Assembly of the UNESCO in Paris.

The theme for the Inter-American sessions to be held in Valparaíso was *Greater Understanding Between Latin America and the United States.* In Spanish the title was *Integración americana.*

The seven important universities of Chile, the Department of State of the United States, and the OAS were the sponsoring entities. Since the Chilean universities were having their annual vacations at the time of the sessions, many of the professors were able to contribute with their presence and several gave lectures concerning the problems and their solutions.

The sessions concluded on January 26, 1963. It was soon after the end of these, during the period of evaluation and planning for other similar meetings, that Dr. Marin suffered the attack that put an end to his brilliant career as diplomat and writer. At first it did not seem that the stroke he suffered would be fatal. He was hospitalized and had the best medical attention available. Doña Milena was making plans to have him moved back to his home in Santiago when his condition suddenly worsened; on February 10 he peacefully left this life a few days before his sixty-third birthday. His death was attributed to a combination of high blood pressure and incipient ulcers. And as during their lives together, Doña Milena was constantly at his side comforting him through his sickness and demise.

Considering Dr. Marin's many contributions to Inter-American and even to world culture it is not strange that innumerable organizations had special meetings to pay homage to him and to his work. One of the most meaningful memorial services was sponsored by the Pan American Union and held on March 20, 1963. Dr. Mora, General Secretary, introduced the theme of the session:

> We are gathered in the American Room to pay homage to an illustrious Chilean who stood out in many varied aspects of culture, literature, and medical science, a man who illustrated the classical sentence, "Nothing of interest to humanity is foreign to me."
>
> Dr. Marin was American by birth but universal through his experiences and knowledge. His memory will last through the centuries as that of a spirit that gave impulse to all of those ideals that unite the people of America.
>
> On beginning his new career with the OAS, after having

been active in medicine and diplomacy, . . . he was able to initiate a new period in his life as a man enamored of humanism.

. . . .

He tried to eliminate the two most formidable barriers that tend to oppose cultural rapprochement: the lack of understanding between various cultures being the first and the second unequal elevation of the social levels in this same culture. We all know how much he did to eliminate these two barriers through education, belles lettres, music, plastic arts, and bibliography. . . .

With his customary penetration in one of his recent articles he commented that the people of the world may be divided into two camps: those who know and those who do not. He estimated that two-fifths of the world's population belong to the second division. . . . He pointed out the urgency of enlightening this group.

. . . .

In fomenting the various forms of culture he also struggled in the cause of liberty. He had the profound conviction that the essential characteristic of America is its identification with liberty.

. . . .

Juan Marin displayed the energetic signs of the Chilean nationality, derived, apparently, from an austere geography closed in between the sea and mountains, a rugged aptitude spurred on by a viril force that does not admit of defeat.

In the years in which I had the good fortune to enjoy his friendship, I came to know the man, a man of principles and ideals exemplified in Juan Marin.

. . . .

We find with us the companion of his struggles and dreams, Doña Milena Luksic de Marin. In her strong personality we know that Juan will continue to survive.

. . . .

The tireless navigator whose character was formed in the harsh regions of South Chile, enamored by limitless horizons, continued his journey into the cultures of both the Orient and the Occident. He now sets out toward the unknown, abandoning us on the shore of the mysterious sea. But his example and his work will continue lighting the way for the present and the future generations of America.[28]

It is, however, from a discourse by the late Muna Lee, an intimate and long-time friend of the Marins, that we take the most concise statement of Dr. Marin's qualities and contributions.

> *Americanist* is a relatively new word in both English and Spanish. You will not find it in all dictionaries; and those that include it are not always in agreement as to its meaning. With regard to Dr. Juan Marin, we must apply the most ample definition, that of the *Oxford Dictionary,* which defines an Americanist as "one who makes a special study of subjects pertaining to America: as its geology, natural history, ethnology, antiquities, history, or resources." And with regard to Dr. Juan Marin, even that wide definition is not wide enough, since it fails to specify that insofar as he is concerned, "resources" include "human resources"—always of the utmost importance to him—and it fails to include specifically a study of America's spiritual aspects, a study of the heart and soul of man in America, as well as the nature of his environment and the record of his activities. The Americanist interest of Juan Marin was total.
>
> "Culture and freedom," he declared, "in my opinion indivisible, are basic to inter-American understanding. The fundamental condition for cultural development of the American people is possession of spiritual freedom and political democracy."
>
> Once when asked what concept of his he would most like to have regarded as his own ideological contribution to the Pan American Union, Juan Marin replied, "I would wish that with the passage of the years there remain indelibly impressed the truth of what I have always been fighting for—the absolute, strict identification of culture with the concept of freedom."[29]

One citation that is a great source of pride to Mrs. Marin is the following:

> [Senator] Mr. Morse: Mr. President, Mr. Richard Butrick, a retired Foreign Service officer residing in the District of

Columbia, has informed me of the death in Chile of Dr. Juan Marin.

Dr. Marin's passing is a genuine loss to the United States. On December 8, 1941, while serving as Chilean Chargé d'Affaires in China, he immediately offered his services in representation of the several hundred Americans, both official and private, and their interests in Shanghai, and carried on in that capacity, at considerable personal danger from inflamed Japanese, until the U. S. Government several weeks later appointed the Swiss Government as its official representative.

Dr. Marin, whose broad-faceted career included service as a doctor, naval officer, and distinguished diplomat representing Chile in China, India, Egypt, and El Salvador and as a distinguished contemporary writer, at the time of his death was on leave from his position as Director of Cultural Affairs of the Organization of American States and serving as director of the summer school of the University of Chile, which was dedicating this session to a study of inter-American relations and the operation of the Alliance for Progress.

In his many posts abroad and in Washington since 1956, Dr. Marin and his wife Milena established a wide circle of devoted American friends who will greatly miss him and whose sorrow at his passing merges with that of his widow.[30]

Secretary of State Rusk in a telegram sent to Doña Milena expressing his condolences said:

One of my predecessors, Cordell Hull, had a special reason to thank Dr. Marin who assumed charge of the interests of the United States in China in 1941 as well as the protection of many North American lives. Your husband was always with us. He was a strong uniting force of friends between his beloved Chile and the United States.

He furnished a continuing link of friendship beginning with the first days of the Second World War until the time of his tragic death that surprised him in the midst of a new struggle in this hemisphere—in this decade—for the progress of its peoples.

Please accept the sincere condolences of my wife and

> mine and with them those of your many friends in the
> Department of State.[31]

Many special memorial meetings were held in various parts of the world and so many letters, cables, and telegrams of condolence were received by Mrs. Marin that a mere listing of them would occupy pages. Doña Milena has kept only the most significant of these but even months after her husband's death there came from remote corners of the world belated letters expressing the feeling of loss of someone that the Marins had met in their travels. Soon after the passing of Dr. Marin two honors in the way of educational scholarships and centers established in his name came to Dr. Marin.[32]

Although Doña Milena has carefully collected copies of all of her husband's books, articles, and pamphlets that have come to her notice, she has been very helpful by allowing us to examine everything, with the reservation that nothing be taken from her home, even overnight, unless she has at least one duplicate copy. She has, however, been very generous with Juan Marin's other library items, having given over two hundred of these to the Columbus Memorial Library at the Pan American Union. She has presented many important books to the Institute of Chilean Studies[33] in Santiago and has spent weeks visiting second-hand book stores in Santiago and Valparaíso looking for her husband's out-of-print works to donate to the library of Congress. Several items that we were unable to find, e.g. *Poliedro médico, Orestes y yo,* and *Ensayos freudianos,* she has discovered and made available to us with the understanding that eventually they will be given to the Library of Congress or some other important collection.

Stendhal is supposed to have remarked: "A hundred years from now readers will recognize my work and begin to take an interest in it." It is much too early for even the most daring critic to attempt to assign to Dr. Juan Marin—poet, fiction writer, and author of an infinity of other types of works—his permanent place. From his earliest days he felt a deep urge to write. He could have been a great professor of philosophy, literature, sociology, or medicine, for he was one of those, to quote Chaucer, "Who would gladly learn and gladly teach." But he evidently felt that his teaching could be done better through the printed page.

Dr. Marin, although the most open-minded person imaginable, was quite aware of the great contributions of Christianity, but he found in the religious philosophies of the Far East, especially in those of India, suggestions and concepts that are designed to help man understand his world and himself. Open-mindedness and intellectual curiosity are essential to better solutions to the philosophical and religious problems that will always confront humanity. Although millions accept with faith a solution that has already been reached, questing minds, such as that of Juan Marin, will continue to ask: why? where? and how?, and will struggle to find what they feel are even more satisfactory answers to these age-old questions.

We would not classify Dr. Marin as an orator. We have heard him speak effectively and convincingly before relatively large audiences, but he was at his best with more intimate groups when he could use a conversational style; he seemed to prefer to maintain a close physical, mental, and spiritual relationship with his hearers. We were on one occasion invited by Doña Milena to listen to a recording that he had been persuaded to prepare. His presentation was that of a conversationalist, of the deep thinker, of the professor. Although his voice, on the recordings, was clear and well modulated, he seemed to feel the need of the more personal contacts that a lover of humanity depends on so much.

Dr. Marin was a good listener, which is, of course, typical of the successful diplomat as well as of the friendly counselor. In small groups of five to ten persons where the interchange of ideas was easily obtained, he was at his best. In such groups he did not insist, as do many profound thinkers, on directing the conversations but would, from time to time, ask pertinent questions, questions that revealed the thinker who gives importance to what others say. Too many of our facile orators are prone to emphasize their facility instead of concentrating on more thoughtful and more straightforward expression.

Unfortunately Dr. Marin was a bit reticent when asked to make recordings of his own writings. While reading and rereading his best poems, for example, "Mecánica," "Buenos Aires," or "Atlantic cabaret," we tried, in vain, to imagine how they would sound read by their author in his deep but well modulated voice. We, like many others, regretted his delay in making the recordings often proposed by his admirers. What a treasure his own oral interpretation of choice selections of his prose and poetry would have been! Had he been blessed with the three score and ten years that the Bible mentions as our legitimate heritage, would he have finally provided us with this treasure? We can only guess, but maybe he would have preferred to leave to us the oral interpretation of his written words.

CHAPTER II

Poetry

Although such great novels as *Paralelo 53 sur (Parallel 53 South)*[1] and *Viento negro (Black Wind)*[2] have induced many critics to give limited attention to Dr. Marin's poetry, we feel that it deserves a chapter even in our brief study.

Like many masters of prose, Juan Marin was, at a very early age, attracted to poetry. His first poems were written while he was attending the *Liceo de Talca* (The Talca secondary school) from 1910 to 1914. In a book published by Roberto Meza Fuentes, *El jardín profanado (The Desecrated Garden,* 1916)[3], there is included some of Juan Marin's earliest verse. Also in the literary magazines *Revista aliados* (1917)[4] and *Selva lírica* (1917)[5] one finds some of his youthful efforts. We shall limit ourselves to a very brief evaluation of two relatively thin volumes, *Looping*[6] and *Aquarium*[7], and one isolated poem "Atlantic cabaret" published in a special edition of the *Diario latino*[8] of San Salvador, El Salvador.

LOOPING

This book of verse consists of sixteen poems with a total of 118 pages. Most of the items had been published previously in magazines[9] and newspapers[10] in Santiago and in *PROA*,[11] a literary review edited in Buenos Aires partly under the leadership and the inspiration of the eminent novelist, author of *Don Segundo Sombra*, Ricardo Güiraldes, a friend of the Marins.

Following the suggestions of his friends and admirers, Juan Marin decided to assemble sixteen of these poems in a volume, giving it the name of one of the best selections, "Looping." A reference to our *Biography* will remind the reader that this was published after he had left for England. Elementary errors convince us that Dr. Martin did not give his personal attention to the printing of *Looping*.

Unfortunately, *Looping* received much less attention than it deserved when it appeared in the book stores of Santiago. It was received much better in other Spanish American countries and in Europe than in Chile.[12]

Much is made of the form of the poems in *Looping*. They resemble some of the poems of Walt Whitman; they do not depend on rhyme or meter, as usually understood, for their musicality. In fact Dr. Marin was often considered by critics to be a *vanguardista*.

As in the case with any casual reader, we have enjoyed all of the poems in this collection but because of our spiritual preparation and past experiences, we have reacted more strongly to those having to do with aviation. We are sure that the poet was emotionally exalted in all sixteen poems; it is evident that aviation, at that time, was very exciting and thrilling to him. It is easy to speculate on the fact that the collection takes its title from the last poem of the group, "Looping." The first poem dedicated to flight instructor Alfredo Puga is also about aviation.

Spin[13]

In "Spin" there are found many expressions showing vividly the pilot's emotions, which the author used to evoke the reader's sympathetic understanding. Perhaps the first four lines which are repeated again later in the poem as a sort of refrain are most typical:

> Song . . . . oh Song
> of steel this morning
> cut in a hundred golden slices
> and wrapped in cotton bandages.[14]

The poem ends leaving the reader emotionally suspended:

> LIFE
>   blue sadism
>   full of pain
>   making a mockery of events

52

                    EARTH
                         open
                              for broken fuselages
                                        with a GOOD BYE
                    and the SPIRIT free
                              playing hide and seek
                                   with the sun . . . .[15]

Superavión

This second poem concerning aviation, although still appealing
to the emotions, has a more subdued tone possibly because it is
dedicated to the memory of a fellow aviator who had recently died:

> Above the spring-board of the virgin winds
> the metal butterfly has leapt
> a pilot heart departs to hunt constellations
> tetrahelic goggles, leather jacket for the adventure
>
>   rrrrrrrrrr   .   .   .
> It has lost itself in endless forces
> the heart of man goes on
> and on
> climbing in infinite vertices
> on the screen of the universe
> signs are projected
> astral cries
> are born, break and die in themselves
> beyond the lines in the dances of small horizons
> and microscopic centuries
> beyond the stars, above the dust
> of the constellations' atomic gold
> above the gallop of ideologies
> in the midst of the shadows of the Cosmos
> Man confirms his millenary existence
> with the Superplane of his mind.[16]

Looping

Here the poet returns to the theme of "Spin." Again we experience the emotional reenactment of the pilot's thrills of doing
rolls, spins, and loops:

Flying above 5000 metres
I planned a looping this morning
I took Saxophone with me
a black pekinese who is my mascot
and my only preoccupation[17]

. . . . . .

we are at 3000 oh! how far we are from
God's Kingdom[18]

. . . . . .

but it is time to descend
let's dive
and say goodbye
      on earth
everything will be the same
the house
     the buses
        Marion[19]

Lieutenant Puga took a special interest in this young surgeon who beyond the call of duty wished to learn to fly a plane. After several hours of instruction, he certified his student, Juan Marin, for solo flying.

We can picture the poet in "Spin" or "Looping" going out to the flying field early in the morning to practice aerobatics. After half an hour or maybe an hour of dives, rolls, and loops, he returns to his room to put down on paper his emotional reactions to his temporary escape from reality.

Boxing

In 1923 Dr. Marin was appointed Chief Doctor of the *Federación de Box de Chile*. He had many opportunities to learn all about "the manly sport of self-defense." His keen observation is shown in his poem "Boxing":

Cameras, buckets, sponges
men in cap and white vest
ultracivilized apache faces
officiating in acts of magic
in the corners of the ring-side[20]

> Arms that end in black tumors
> line of flesh in the air
> dance of biceps and legs
> on guard . . . up! . . . uppercut!!![21]

Buenos Aires

This is dedicated to Ricardo Güiraldes. On reading this poem, we were reminded of Walt Whitman and Carl Sandburg, both of whom found poetry in the palpitating heart of a great city. Juan Marin, as an indefatigable and omnivorous reader was without doubt acquainted with these two most original American writers.

Yankilandia

"Yankilandia" (dedicated to Jack Dempsey), a companion piece to "Buenos Aires," does not reach the lyrical level of the latter. This poem in less than three pages, eight stanzas of five lines each, gives a word picture of the materialistic successes of the United States. It is possible that by deserting his favorite form, a form untrammelled by meter or rhyme, Dr. Marin lost something of his inspiration. What is the unusual construction of "Yankilandia"? A scanning of the forty-one lines of this intriguing poem shows that the author planned the following scheme: each of the stanzas begins with four un-rhymed eleven syllable lines; seven of the eight end with a climactical line of seven or eleven syllables; only with the final stanza does he put in an extra short six syllable line.

Navy

In the poem "Navy" we imagine that Dr. Marin is describing a short trip on the *Baquedano* one afternoon with visitors aboard.

Klaxon

This expresses vividly the emotional reactions of the driver of a powerful automobile.

Oceanic Film

Dedicated to the Maule region, Dr. Marin's native land, "Oceanic Film" seems to be a song in praise of the many *maulinos* who have gone to sea. The last four lines with their 6-6-6-5 syllables to the verse represent the coming of the Valkyries to call the *maulinos* to the sailor's life.

Nightclubs and Entertainers

In "Sonyeuse," "Bataclán," "Josephine Baker," "Shimmy," "Wamp," and "Leona," the poet has used night-club scenes. "Shimmy" is one of the best examples from the group of the modernistic techniques in painting applied to poetry. The reader catches fleeting glimpses of form and meaning only to be startled to find new and unrelated elements brought in.

Fox-Trot

"Fox-Trot" presents emotionally and poetically a dance that for a while was the obsession of the entire world:

> Music which
> has the strange rhythm of mechanical things
> in time with the waves beneath the hydroplanes
> or the rhythm of
> the systoles or diastoles
> electro-cardiac-dynamic
> of hearts[22]
>
> . . . .
>
> Fox-trot
> divine dance of Mr. and Miss
> in a gigantic advance
> such as Attila's or Nimrod's
> you swept from Washington to Paris
> We dance you like articulated marionettes
> the soul all yours is a muscular spring
> arms and legs entwined
> and intermixed
> like the waves of the sea

> when you enter the dance halls
> one catches a whiff of gas
> and a tinkle of glass
> on bar counters
> remnants of Municipal bands
> dance in the orchestration
> the dissonant music is mad
> a negro with springs in his mouth
> breaks his own record on the trombone!![23]

ATLANTIC CABARET

The poem "Atlantic cabaret" was not included in *Looping* but belongs to the same period. Its first publication, according to a critical article by Orestes Plath, "Itinerario trunco de Juan Marin," was in *Gong* of Valparaíso in 1930 but we have used for our study the reprinting in *Diario latino*. Juan Marin captured the atmosphere of the famous international night club when the naval vessel *Almirante Latorre* passed through the Panama Canal on its way to England in 1929. To illustrate the poet's picture of an evening in this cabaret, we give a few extracts. "Atlantic cabaret" which came between the two publications *Looping* and *Aquarium* was one of the author's favorites.

> Atlantic cabaret
> of Colón:
> acrobatic sailors dancing
> O.K. . . ! O.K. . . !
> The saxophone,
> the fox, the conga, rhumba and black-bottom
> and the danzón. . . .
>   . . . .
> Faces show white teeth
> and sweat
> All the rhythm and syncopation
> of today.
>   . . . .
> The dollars sing on the glasses
> with their lyrical song of engines!
> Girls of Hawaii
> girls of Luzon

legs from Broadway and the Philippines
from Sydney and Saigon.

. . . .

Merceditas, girl of Jamaica
let us drink our quiet sherry
and dance the fox,
and later, when dawn tinges the sky,
let us say goodbye.

. . . .

Merceditas, dark-skinned girl of Jamaica
daughter of Africa, born
in the lands of Christopher Columbus. . . . !

. . . .

Little taxi girl without country, without
a past, without God.[24]

AQUARIUM

Comparing the poems in *Looping* with those in this second and shorter collection, *Aquarium,* one notes that the latter are more restrained, more sophisticated, and more carefully constructed. The years that had elapsed since the poems of *Looping* were written had changed Dr. Marin's way of looking at the world.

Instead of taking up the poems as they appear in the published volume, we propose to follow this order:

a) *"Mecánica"*

b) *Five maritime poems:*   "Mancha cromática" - "Nocturno" - "Paisaje" - "Matinal" - "Zarpe"

c) *Five short, five line poems:*   "Farol" - "Sinfonía blanca" - "Sinfonía roja" - "Amanecer" - "Marítima"

d) *"Era"*

Mecánica

This poem has been given great importance by critics, rightly we believe, for it seems to be a sort of manifesto, a declaration of poetic liberty. Several critics[25] have studied Marin's poems that dared introduce what had been considered such non-poetic subjects as: aviation, night clubs, boxing, automobiles, cities, and personalities. An important critical article written by Orestes Plath mentions other poets who have used such subjects: "Thus in Juan Marin . . . one finds a zeal for mechanical things . . ."[26] No one has given the precise manifesto found in Marin's "Mecánica."

> Oh poem of steel that enfolds the new world
> cry of the factory's bronchial tubes
> your rhymes are beveled axes
> resplendent with dynamic will
>   . . . . .
> machinery song and system
> hidden philosophy of an unknown alchemy
> a Man will appear
> who will show you nude
> who will penetrate your secrets
> pour your heart in your retorts
> burn it in your furnaces
> and write
> the new poetry
> that of straight lines
> and fuselages
> of high aerials
> and the infinitely swift wheels
> that move you[27]
>   . . . . .

Juan Marin did not believe, of course, that one must desert the "Lamb and the Tree," i.e. bucolic themes, but that rather some new subjects ought to be employed.

Five Maritime Poems

These poems deserve more extensive treatment but only one, "Zarpe," is presented with a very short paraphrasing; a fairly long quotation will be found in our *General Notes:*

The sky has gone so high
for it has dropped the ballast of its clouds . . .

. . . . .

Night is lighting up
        its fires
in its black boilers
    Sparks fly whirling toward heaven
and it *SETS ITS PROW TOWARD THE DAWN*[28]

Five Poems of Five Lines Each

These are, without doubt, some of Juan Marin's best poems, but their very shortness denies them the attention that "Buenos Aires," for example, will always receive. The poems remind us of some of the Japanese poetry that was quite popular in Spanish America during the first decades of the Twentieth Century. Without maintaining their artificiality, insofar as number of syllables is concerned, they could be a mixture of the *tanka* and the *haikai*. The chief virtue of the Japanese poems is the simple, one-thought unity, especially in the *haikai*. Dr. Marin has made the unity of each more pronounced by repeating the first line of each poem again as the fifth. We include translations of four of them made by Carlos and Esther Vallejo: "Sinfonía blanca" (White Symphony), "Sinfonía roja" (Red Symphony), "Amanecer" (Dawn), and "Marítima" (Sea Coast).

White Symphony

A skeleton dances in the snow
  White as a dream
    And the moon wraps it around
      And shadows its bones in blue
        A skeleton dances in the snow.[29]

Red Symphony

In the fiery sunset
  A stray butterfly hovers
    Its diminutive red veil
      Caresses like a tongue
        In the fiery sunset[30]

Dawn

Bird's song at sunrise
  Melodious footlight
    Music with which to shoot
     The soul of the grove
      Bird's song at sunrise[31]

Sea Coast

Glaucous wave that ebbs and flows
  Caresses and menaces
    That stretches out one snowy thigh
     And retreats toward the dawn
      Glaucous wave that ebbs and flows[32]

Era

This last poem from *Aquarium* is possibly the most subject to varied interpretations but is it not a truly great love song? The title may well be translated "Once upon a time" or simply "Long ago" for Spanish fairy tales often begin "Erase que se era" (Once upon a time). Is this the poet's memory, somewhat nostalgic, of a night spent with a girl who in spite of being "a butterfly with clipped wings" or "a rose fallen from its vase" comes back to haunt her erstwhile lover whose memory reconstructs her in all of her youthful and pristine purity?

In his prologue to this study Dr. Fernando Alegría calls attention to Chilean *creacionismo*.[33] At times in *Looping* and more often in *Aquarium* Juan Marín makes use of but seldom misuse of this *ism*. Note from "Era": "sus pestañas antenas" (her eyelashes antennas), "sus ojos de aquarium" (her aquarium eyes), and "su alma vestida de lluvia" (her soul dressed with rain). If, however, we compare "Era" with "Atlantic cabaret" we find that even in his poems Dr. Marín is at his best when he has a story to tell.

In conclusion we should like to suggest that, except for "Mecánica" which might well have been a part of *Looping*, the poems of *Aquarium* are more subdued, less discordant. It is possible that when Juan Marín made his break from the Parnasianism of his earlier verse he felt the need for a more strident production. Only with the passing of many years will the critic be able to decide which of these two volumes has more lasting values.

Chile may rightly be called "The Land of Poets." Gabriela Mistral, Pablo Neruda, and Pablo Rokha, to mention only these three, have won world-wide acceptance. Had Dr. Marin continued to dedicate himself to verse, he would have received as much praise for his poetry as he has for his fictional writing. As we discuss his prose productions we shall note that almost invariably he illustrated his presentation of the great literatures of Tibet, China, Egypt and India with his own translations to Spanish verse.[34]

CHAPTER III

Prose Fiction and Drama

In spite of the undisputed beauty of Dr. Marin's poetry pointed out in Chapter II, he will probably be better remembered for his prose fiction, at least for the present. We do not, of course, believe that he will be forgotten as a poet, but most people when his name is mentioned will exclaim immediately, "Oh yes, the author of *Paralelo 53 sur (Parallel 53 South)* and of *Viento negro (Black Wind)!*"[1]

We propose to discuss Juan Marin's prose fiction in three sections: Short Stories, Novelettes, and Novels. No pretense is made to maintain a rigid chronological order but because the novelist, especially in Spanish America, begins with shorter compositions, chronology will not be seriously violated.

The first date we have for a published short story by Juan Marin is October 7, 1921—"Héroes anónimos" (Anonymous Heroes).[2] The Santiago, Chile newspaper, *La Nación,* had held a short story contest and Dr. Marin's winning story was published on the first page. It is accepted as a fact that the short story has become very popular in Chile and that this genre has reached great artistic heights. One of the main outlets for this literary form is the Sunday edition of two of the leading newspapers, *El Mercurio* and *La Nación.* Many other newspapers and various magazines also publish short stories. The outstanding critico-literary publication of the University of Concepción, *Atenea,* uses some creative writing; Juan Marin's story, "El derrumbe del cielo," appeared in its pages.

A selection of his most popular stories that had appeared in newspapers and magazines was made by Dr. Marin and issued as a book under the title *Alas sobre el mar*[3] *(Wings Over the Sea)* in 1934. This was his second book of prose fiction, the first having been *Margarita, el aviador y el médico (Margaret, the Aviator, and the Doctor).*[4]

Section I

THE SHORT STORIES

Dr. Marin has written very few really brief short stories of the kind made popular in Spain by Blasco Ibáñez and Pardo Bazán. He did not choose to present his characters with merely two or three sentences. Being a keen observer and very much interested in people, he enjoyed introducing them carefully and in detail, both physically and psychologically. He preferred beginning a story slowly, putting the reader into a relaxed attitude, and later speeding up the action. The vignette or the story-complete-on-this-page has had little vogue in Spanish America.

ALAS SOBRE EL MAR

(Wings Over the Sea)

This collection, now out of print, has an excellent *Prólogo (Prologue)* by the well known novelist and close friend of Juan Marin, Salvador Reyes. Although Salvador Reyes is remembered more for his novels, most of which have their setting in or near Valparaíso, Chile, he has demonstrated his critical insight in such books as *Rostros sin máscaras.*[5]

We find the date, probably that of their first printing, indicated at the beginning of all but three of the fifteen *cuentos* (tales) of the collection, the earliest being 1926. As noted above, however, our author had won a prize in 1921 with his "Héroes anónimos," which unfortunately does not appear in either of his two volumes of *cuentos.* It is quite probable that several additional compositions, not collected in book form, will be found eventually. The latest date assigned to any story in this collection is 1933, shortly before *Alas sobre el mar* appeared.

According to Dr. Marin's own statement, the short novel *Margarita* . . . (1932) was finished in 1930 while he was in Paris. Because several of the *cuentos* in *Alas* . . . have their setting in Europe, we presume that they were written at the same time that he was working on *Margarita*. . . . In the following pages we shall discuss all fifteen as they appear in this collection.

Un raid a través del misterio (A Flight into Mystery)[6]

Here there are many elements of the fantastic although the descriptions are quite realistic. Eliminating the carefully worked out background of Dr. Marin's depiction of planes, the sea, and the beautiful coast line of Chile, we have the following simple narrative:

Several groups of aviators are asked to set out in their hydroplanes on an exploratory trip. Our raconteur, a physician, is in a plane that is forced down in the rough sea near the coast. The one remaining engine has power enough to taxi them to shore. The doctor, who acts also as quartermaster, looking for food and lodging, is stopped by a young lady who says her sister needs medical attention, but that it would be better to return later to examine her for she is just coming out of a trance.

The first hint of the fantastic is: How did this young lady know of the arrival of the aviators and how did she know that this man was a doctor? We learn then that the sick girl, when in trance, is clairvoyant and that she can transmit messages through telepathy. After dinner the doctor goes to see her accompanied by some of the crew, including lieutenant Herrera. When the girl sees Herrera, she has a premonition of his coming death.

The mechanics have repaired the second engine and they finally take off but the engine fails again. This time their landing is not so fortunate and only three of the crew are saved. Herrera is one of those lost. Investigations offer no scientific explanation of the strange events that are happening. Dr. Marin, although fundamentally a man of science, always had an open mind when faced with psychic phenomena.

El hombre del funeral (The Man at the Funeral)

Technically this is one of Juan Marin's best short stories. The raconteur goes one afternoon to a funeral of somebody who died the night before while at a party where narcotics and strange intoxicating beverages were being served. As his carriage was departing, an old man (who was dressed in a mourning cloak and was carrying an umbrella) climbed in. His conversation, a monologue rather, dealt with different peculiar theories such as the existence of the non-existent and the way empty spaces in the world are filled by the dead. On his way back from the cemetery, trying to avoid the company of the odd man, our raconteur invited a friend to ride with him so that they could discuss his recent experiences, for he was greatly intrigued as to the identity of his erstwhile companion.

His friend insisted that he had been riding behind in another carriage and that he had not seen any mysterious stranger. After listening to the description of the peculiar man it became clear that he was the man just buried.

Nupcial (Nuptial)

"Nupcial" is the tragic story of a young pilot who flies out to visit his fiancée, accompanied by a friend who never wanted to fly. At a farewell party that the navy gave for some pilots, everybody insisted that Lieutenant Bazán should see his girl friend before leaving for the South. It was only a twenty minute flight. The group commander gave permission for them to make the trip, and the crowd drank to the happiness of the young couple.

Next morning the two friends left the home of the fiancée where Lieutenant Bazán had become formally engaged. On the return trip they became lost in a fog; the plane crashed against the mountains and fell into a lake. The young fiancée, lying in her bed day-dreaming about the happiness she had just shared with Bazán, was suddenly overcome by a great anguish. She imagined that she saw a plane taking the shape of a black cross falling into a dark sea. This is an additional bit of evidence of Dr. Marin's interest in extrasensory perception.

En el límite (The Close Call)

Some flying officers are talking in the casino of the death of one of their companions which had occurred that same afternoon in a plane accident. They insist that Lieutenant Romero tell them about his own impressions when his plane crashed and fell into shallow water during maneuvers. After some hesitation he tells them that his arms were caught on the body of the plane and that at first he could not free himself. During those few seconds of acute suffering until he was rescued he fought for his life, trying not to breathe, knowing that otherwise he would be drowned.

Hole haven

This is the name of an English pub on the banks of the Thames River opposite the pier where ships anchor while loading explosives. A young Chilean officer goes to the pub every night to chat with the owner and with his beautiful daughter named Marjorie. When he asks permission to take the girl out for a visit to London (with which she is not acquainted) the father's answer is yes; he thinks he can let her go with the Chilean gentleman but not tonight because it is rather late. Some other day! Tonight the officer will be his guest, his first in many years, and they will talk. He wishes to tell him a story.

"Three generations of Simpsons have owned this tavern. My great grandfather was the first. My grandfather was twice married. By his second wife he had a very beautiful daughter, like mine, also called Marjorie. For some time a Japanese ship was anchored exactly where yours is now. Every night her Captain would come in for drinks. Late one night this Japanese Captain came, tied up my grandfather, and took Marjorie out to the ship. When my father came back, he wanted to call the police, but my grandfather, wishing to take revenge for the dishonor to his family, rowed out to the Japanese ship, blew her up, and killed everybody on board—including Marjorie."

La historia del amor del Dr. Jerkins (Dr. Jerkins' Love Story)

Dr. Jerkins, being asked by a group to tell his love story, recalls an adventure of his youth when, feeling a bit lonely, he made the acquaintance of a very beautiful girl. He passed several hours with her in a most intimate companionship. A few days later, while visiting a colony of lepers, the colony doctor pointed out to him a new inmate. His former girl friend!! Although this is an old theme, we feel that Dr. Marin has treated it exceptionally well.

La extraña aventura del estudiante Propoulos
(Student Propoulos' Strange Adventure)

Propoulos, after several hours of celebration with much wine and strong drink, takes a long walk in an old part of London. He is accosted by a woman, a street walker, who insists on taking him to her apartment. After more drinks he decides to leave, but she will not let him go. During the struggle he loses consciousness. When he comes to his senses, he finds that he is in the police station. There is no sign of the house to which Propoulos says he was taken. Only a slip of paper is found in his pocket with the cryptic message:

Miss Medusa of the Night

Hell-Park, London

A través de la noche (As the Ship Was Sinking)

This is unusually appealing to us, for not too long ago we made the trip from Valparaíso to Punta Arenas (formerly Magallanes) along the coast stopping at Talcahuano, Ancud, Puerto Montt, and Aysen, and on across the Golfo de Penas. Juan Marin, as do so many of his fellow Chilean writers, makes just enough use of local color to give a suggestion of realism to his otherwise imaginative fiction.

Among the characters introduced by Juan Marin there were a beautiful lady who is a student pianist at the Conservatory of Santiago and an unkempt old man who joins the passengers at a channel port. A storm develops; most of the trip is made by following the inner passages. But as they enter the open sea into the Golfo de Penas, the storm gets worse. Though the Captain has ordered them all to their cabins, the passengers insist on remaining in the dining room. The pianist agrees to play. The old man, who has been drinking, feasts his eyes on her. When someone grasps him by the shoulders and angrily shakes him, he is found to be dead. The ship sinks while the young lady, who seems to be in a trance, continues to play.

Pop's Club

The raconteur is a Spanish American who has been invited to join a private night club in London, where all the waitresses are exceedingly beautiful as are the members of the all-girl orchestra. When he shows too much interest in the pianist, he is asked to leave by Old Patrick, the owner.

A few days later the girl comes to his hotel. They pledge everlasting love. The young man has to go back home for a short trip but his return is delayed for two years. When he finds the girl, he discovers that she has become one of the lowest of streetwalkers. After some hesitation she explains that Old Patrick has those beautiful girls for his own pleasure. Any girl who refuses his attention or who takes up with another man is dismissed and through his influence is not given work at any other night club. The young man takes the girl, who is quite ill, to a local hospital where she soon dies.

El 'Curco' Meléndez (The Hunch-back Meléndez)

This is one of Dr. Marin's stories depicting student life in the medical school. A certain Pereda representing his school fraternity offers himself as a spy to discover the secrets of another fraternity. He tries to do it by giving money to the poorest of the students of that group, Meléndez, who pretends acceptance of it. Meléndez invites Pereda to attend an initiation ceremony taking place that night, the climax of which is to drink a concoction from a human skull. But he will have to go through the entire ceremony blindfolded. Everyone is going to wear a hood! When Pereda's time comes up and he is drinking, he feels something terrible going through his throat. He screams, throwing away the skull in horror, while Meléndez is shouting, "I put a tape-worm in his drink!!"

La promesa del Capitán Ulrici (Captain Ulrici's Promise)

"Captain Ulrici's Promise" has a fantastic element bordering on spiritualism. Annoyed at the cold materialism of a young pilot, Captain Ulrici offers to make one of those agreements so often read about in relation with spiritism. At the time of his death and before any news of it can possibly reach his skeptical friend, Ulrici will find a way of letting him know. On coming back from a flight the young pilot seems to lose control of his plane that apparently is headed for a crash into the sea. Just at the last minute, however, some mysterious power takes control, levels off the plane and lands it safely. The doubting young pilot learns that at that same minute Ulrici has died in a crack-up.

El hombre de medianoche (The Man From Midnight)

Among other interesting techniques, Juan Marin uses one with a weird or far-out assumption. In "El hombre de medianoche" the premise is that a person may live in time as well as in space; only a chosen few live in time. Among those living in midnight (medianoche) are Dante, Poe, and Rodin. The raconteur already deep in his cups is accosted by a stranger who, after explaining the existence of time-citizens, says that his homeland is midnight. The hour is eleven-thirty and the two are sitting in O'Sullivan's pub. The stranger says that he will have to leave at the stroke of twelve for, although the time-citizens may visit other hours, they are at home only in their own zones. As the bar-room clock begins to strike twelve midnight, our "Hombre de medianoche" arises, shakes hands, and says good-bye. Dr. Marin makes use of this technique in a few additional stories. (See "El hombre de música.")

Año 2000 (*The Year 2000*)

"Año 2000" assumes that the year 2000 has arrived. Only a few nations have lived through the Twentieth Century's struggles for supremacy. The government for the Western Hemisphere is based in Havana, Cuba. Japan, however, has not entered into this world conference. As hundreds of planes of the Western Hemisphere are returning to their countries they discover that Japan is planning to take over the entire world. A group of ten planes decides to destroy the ship of the Japanese admiral by a final suicidal dive!

Au bal colonial (*At the Colonial Club*)

This is the story of a Negro night club in Paris. The flighty and too venturesome girl friend of our raconteur insists on the thrill of going to a very off-beat night club where the entertainers, who are all uncouth, uneducated and physically strong, often forcibly invite the guests to take part in their frantic gyrations. The young man refuses at first, but finally, against his better judgment, offers to escort his friend. As he had feared, a husky Negro drags the girl into the dance, and when her escort tries to rescue her he is knocked out. The next morning she returns to her friends with her dress torn to shreds and her face and body badly beaten. A short time later the offending entertainer is found murdered.

Nocturno marítimo (*Night at Sea*)

A young officer aboard a submarine is traveling south in the Irish Sea on a stormy night. His thoughts are divided between warmer and quieter nights and a girl he has just met. He keeps on hearing her voice and seeing her apparition in the storm. He is sure that she is dead. When he comes to port he hurriedly sends a telegram asking for news of her. But no answer ever comes!

CUENTOS DE VIENTO Y AGUA

Stories of the Sea and Air

Of the fourteen stories in this volume we shall discuss only seven, for the others appear also in *Alas. . . .* It is quite usual for a writer to republish in subsequent collections those tales that have been most favorably accepted previously. We have indicated in our *General Notes* to this chapter that "Un raid através del misterio," discussed with the stories of *Alas . . . ,* was included in this second collection with the title of "Puerto las ánimas."

Puerto negro (Black Port)

This is one of the best Chilean stories to emphasize the miserable lot of the day laborers during the first third of the Twentieth Century. Dr. Marin became more interested in social reform and the fate of the underdogs during his later works but in his short stories he rarely pictures the squalor of the under-privileged.

Two ships, one English and one German, are rushing the loading of coal; the weather is rapidly becoming worse and they wish to leave port as soon as possible. At the end of a shift, a tug-boat towing two barges comes alongside to take the workers to the wharf. Although there is room on the tug for only thirty of the workers, the tug-boat captain takes on board the men from both ships. When the members of the two crews realize too late that they cannot safely ride out the storm with the weight of the two barges in addition to the overload of stevedores, one of them severs the barges' tow-lines thus sacrificing the lives of the men who are on each. Even with the two barges cut loose, the tug-boat, top-heavy with the extra men, turns turtle and all are drowned. After finding the body of his father "el Seco" washed ashore the next morning, Eusebio, the under-sized ten year old son, joins the long line of hopeless miners to become the family wage-earner and thus to await his turn to fall victim to the mines or to the sea.

Several other Chilean writers, for example Mariano Latorre, Salvador Reyes, and Baldomero Lillo, have treated similar scenes and subjects but none has surpassed Dr. Marin's masterly skill in his production of "Puerto negro." *El Mercurio de Santiago* awarded a prize for this story in a contest sponsored in 1937.

Mar Pacífico (Pacific Ocean)

A simple story of man's cruelty to man is herein related. Eight Chinese have paid a ship's purser a large sum of money to smuggle them into Lima, Peru. With the help of the supercargo and a negro deck-hand, the purser, after persuading the trusting Chinese to get into a baggage net to avoid discovery, swings the net over the side of the ship after which he orders the supporting ropes cut; the unsuspecting Chinese drop into the sea. The purser calmly returns to his card game and remarks, *"La banca tiene ocho"* (The bank has eight). Recalling the ill-fated orientals he continues, *"¿Pero este número me persigue esta noche?"* (But is this number to follow me tonight?).

El hombre de música (The Man of Music)

Besides the fantastic element observed in several of Dr. Marin's *cuentos,* the technique of the far-out assumption noted in "El hombre de medianoche" is used here. The premise is that some people are so constituted that their only nourishment is music. The raconteur, attending a concert, is joined by a late-comer who slowly and painfully drags himself into the hall. He seems to be on the verge of fainting. But as soon as the concert begins he commences to show remarkable signs of returning to normal and by the end of the performance he is quite strong and full of vigor. For this person music takes the place of food and drink.

73

Lázaro (Lazarus)

Lazarus, the Biblical character brought back to life by Christ, has been the object of much speculation, of several famous paintings, and of a number of stories. The question that often occurs to anyone reading the Biblical account is, "Could Lazarus have returned to a normal existence to take up his daily routine unaffected by his three days in the Great Beyond?" Brenes Mesén,[7] who had much of the same interest in Far Eastern philosophies and religions that we note in Juan Marin, indicates in his story with the same title that such an experience would certainly change the character of the brother of Martha and Mary of Bethany.

In Dr. Marin's story we are introduced to Massinger who is a painter and also a sculptor. He seems to be thoroughly beset with a desire to portray death. Massinger invites our raconteur and an artist friend to visit his studio where they are introduced to Massinger's sisters, Myriam and Martha. The entire studio is filled with dozens of paintings and statues of death emphasizing the artist's macabre obsession. Massinger begins to expound the theory that an artist is created by his work and not his works by him. The three men finally enter a room where an excellent statue of a reclining young man is displayed. The visitors are amazed by the beauty of the work and say that it must be seen by the public! All at once Massinger sinks back on a bed in the same position as the statue. As the visitors, filled with uncontrollable fright, rush out of the room they hear the two sisters exclaim: "Lazarus, brother, why have you deserted us again?"

El techo del mundo. Fantasía del año 3000
(The Roof Over the World. Fantasy of the Year 3000)[8]

This is as near to science fiction as any story written by Juan Marin. In the year 3000 Earth finds itself being attacked by Mars. To protect Earth, the head scientists decide to build a metal shell over the whole world. The Martians discover a way to destroy this shell and thus to kill all of the inhabitants under it. Then the Martians turn their attention to more important things.

Tifón (Typhoon)

In spite of warnings and the advice of the Port Captain of Kobe, Japan, the commander of a ship insists on going to Shanghai. Almost at once a typhoon hits. Dr. Marin, who had spent some time aboard ships and who had a real love for the sea, describes the storm, the actions of the people who are crazed with fear, and the final entrance of the steamer into the channel leading to Shanghai.

La cacería de un hombre (The Man Hunt)

From the point of view of generally accepted criteria, this is one of the most perfectly constructed of Dr. Marin's short stories. The background of time and place and the introduction of the characters are handled with consummate efficiency and masterly directness. "La cacería . . ." compares favorably with the tales of Maupassant, Poe, or O. Henry and with those of the great Spanish *cuentistas,* Pardo Bazán or Blasco Ibáñez. They contain no unneeded material.

There is trouble in a certain village. Men from neighboring mines arrive in droves on week-ends to spend their money on wine and women. Because of the possible involvement of his soldiers, the commanding officer warns his officers and men to keep away from the village except when on duty. Two young lieutenants disobey the order. When they are caught with a miner's wife, the miner kills one of the lieutenants and seriously wounds the other who reaches camp only to die. The commanding officer gives the murderer a chance to escape so that his soldiers can shoot him; this is the *Ley de la fuga* that allows the guards to kill a captive who is trying to escape.

In conclusion, we repeat that in these seven stories the author has shown great versatility, as well as skill. He goes from the fantastic to the most realistic. In spite of our statement that the very last story discussed, "The Man Hunt," is technically the most perfect of his compositions, Dr. Marin is at his best when he allows himself more time and space for the development of his tales.

OTHER STORIES

The following four stories are examples of the many, published by Juan Marin in newspapers and magazines, that are worthy of inclusion in his collections.

Viaje en el Hurricane (Voyage on the Hurricane)[9]

"Viaje . . ." is more a report of a true happening than a fictional creation but many of Dr. Marin's gifts as a storyteller are found in it. After the Second World War the Marins were furnished transportation for their return to China on a North American ship loaded with high octane gasoline. The constant fear that the ship might be torpedoed and explode is made less nerveracking by the expected birth of a child. All ends happily and Dr. Marin, whose medical practice rarely included obstetrics, helped with the delivery.

Hielos magallánicos en un campo de concentración de Shanghai (The Ice of the Straits of Magellan in a Shanghai Concentration Camp)[10]

Juan Marin reports graphically on the use of his novel, Paralelo 53 sur, to teach Spanish to the prisoners in a Japanese concentration camp in Shanghai.

Héroes anónimos (Anonymous Heroes)

On Friday, October 7, 1921 La Nación, a principal newspaper of Santiago, published this prize winning story, one of Juan Marin's earliest. It is concerned with the work of medical students in one of the Public Assistance centers. People with all kinds of diseases as well as those suffering accidents visit these places at all times of the day or night. A dedicated young medical student in trying to help one of these sufferers is contaminated and dies. Dr. Marin's interest in medicine is never absent from his writings, but this is one of his stories that depends the most on his medical training and experiences.

El derrumbe del cielo[11] *(The Falling of the Skies)*

This story, published in the excellent *Atenea* magazine which is sponsored by the University of Concepción, Chile, shows Dr. Marin's interest in China and his respect for the great teachers that China has produced. A professor surrounded by some of his superior students has been talking about the universe and the power that keeps everything in its place. One of the students asks, "What would happen if the stars should lose their stability and begin to fall?"

The professor cannot conceive of such an occurrence. But as the group, that seems to be meeting on a hill-top overlooking a city, contemplates the possibility, strange lights appear in the sky and swoop down on the sleeping center of population. War planes, probably from Japan, begin to drop heavy bombs. Is the sky really falling? Are the stars losing their stability? The story ends with the professor and the students leaving their hill-top in order to save lives in the city below.

El fondeo (Into the Depths)

In a recent publication *Antología de cuentos chilenos* (Anthology of Chilean Tales),[12] one finds a story "El fondeo" which is a chapter taken from *Paralelo*. . . . It tells of the tragic death by freezing of *el Chilote Grande* (The Big Man from Chiloé) who was locked in a refrigeration plant by the cruel José Alonzo. Frequently parts of novels have been published as short stories either before or after the appearance of the novel. This is, of course, a legitimate practice and many other cuentos could easily be assembled from longer publications.

General Remarks Concerning Juan Marin's Short Stories

In the present section "Short Stories" of the chapter "Prose

Fiction," twenty-six stories have been discussed: fifteen from *Alas sobre el mar,* seven from *Cuentos de viento y agua,* and four that have not been included in either of these two collections. One marvels at the variety represented. Not present in all but occurring quite often is the fantastic element which depends on the supernatural or on extrasensory perception. One might even say that the non-materialistic may be considered our author's principal contribution to this genre. It is clear, however, that when he adhered to the realistic as in "Puerto negro" Dr. Marin is unequalled.[13]

Early in this presentation of the author of *Paralelo 53 sur* there has been quoted the observation of a critic that presupposed that Dr. Marin was looking for his niche and that he was to find it in the novel, the novel that depends on careful observation and that has social significance. But the fact that few anthologies of short stories appear without at least one of Dr. Marin's tales leads us to suggest that had he never written his three major novels, *Paralelo 53 sur, Orestes y yo,* or *Viento negro,* his stories would have assured for him a place in Chilean letters.

Section II

NOVELETTES

Two compositions fall into this second division: *El crimen de Percival Lawrence (Percival Lawrence's Crime)* and *La muerte de Julián Aranda (Julian Aranda's Death).* The first editions of these two novelettes are included in the same volume with *El secreto del Dr. Baloux (Dr. Baloux's Secret),* a novel that we shall discuss later.

This intermediate length category of prose fiction, too long to be classified as a short story and too short to be included with the novels, has been important in Chile. One of the best is Eduardo Barrios' famous *El hermano asno (Brother Donkey)* which has become a classic.

EL CRIMEN DE PERCIVAL LAWRENCE

(Percival Lawrence's Crime)

This is a weird story based on the strange deaths of three members of the Lawrence family who are: father, mother, and Percival—the only son. The raconteur learns that the father, a Protestant missionary established in India and married to the daughter of a very prominent family of that country, had forcibly seduced a priestess of the temple of Siva. After a period of rapid degeneration, Reverend Lawrence died mysteriously but on his throat were seen finger marks, as though he had been strangled.

At the beginning of the story Percival and his mother, a bedridden invalid, are living in England. Percival is a leader of a certain group of Cambridge students; he and our raconteur, a physician, have become very close friends. Percival asks the physician to examine his mother but will not allow her high collar to be unbuttoned. The doctor, however, returns during the son's absence to examine the mother. He discovers finger marks on her neck as though some one had tried to strangle her. Percival calls some time later to say that his mother has died.

It is learned that Percival had renewed an insurance policy on his mother's life for the sum of one hundred thousand pounds just one day before her sudden death. For that reason the company doctor had to examine the deceased. Percival tried to prevent this but was overruled. Marks of strangulation were plainly seen. The son was condemned to be hanged. As Percival was being led to the scaffold he suddenly raised his hands to his neck in pain and was dead before the rope was adjusted for the hanging. The attending physician reported that there were plainly visible marks of strangulation.

LA MUERTE DE JULIAN ARANDA

(Julian Aranda's Death)

The case of a man who is buried alive, recounted herein, reminds one of Poe's *Premature Burial* and *The Fall of the House of Usher*. Juan Marin goes to some lengths to develop the character of Julian Aranda, a man who has always had visions of becoming rich but is not too careful about the legitimacy of the methods; he decides to write his memoirs hoping to make his fortune. In order to increase the sale of the proposed autobiography, Aranda dreams up the idea of being buried alive, supposedly by his enemy, but the burial is in reality carried out by Agatha (the *femme fatale*) and the raconteur, persons that Aranda trusts implicitly. Simultaneously with the supposed crime, news of it is to be sent to the police, to one of the principal newspapers, and to the Ministry of the Interior. In order to keep Aranda alive, two rubber tubes are to lead from the coffin to the open air.

When the police arrive and dig up Aranda they find him dead with evidence of a struggle to escape. The raconteur is accused of murder and is temporarily put into an insane asylum. Agatha has disappeared. Many years later when our raconteur finds Agatha in a hospital on the point of death, she confesses that she had returned to the grave and removed the rubber tubes, in order to eliminate Aranda because he knew too much about her activities as a spy.

Section III

NOVELS

In spite of the artistic qualities of Juan Marin's other writings, we accept the widely held belief that his fame rests primarily on his three novels: *Paralelo 53 sur, Orestes y yo,* and *Viento negro.* Unfortunately many excellent poets, dramatists, and short story writers have their productions in these genres neglected when they write novels that have merited high praise. Among North American writers we note that two of our leading poets, Robert Nathan and Robert Penn Warren, are remembered mainly for their novels. Likewise William Faulkner, whose short stories rank near the top in world literature, is known better for his novels.

Be that as it may, Juan Marin, the poet, the short story writer, and the essayist has given way temporarily to Juan Marin, the novelist.

Dr. Marin has written eight novels: *Margarita, el aviador y el médico; Un avión volaba; Paralelo 53 sur; El secreto del Dr. Baloux; Naufragio; Orestes y yo; Viento negro;* and *Muerte en Shanghai;* these are listed in the order of their publication dates.

According to the author's own statement, *Margarita . . .* was finished in Paris in 1930. He was 29 years of age when he was released from active service in the navy to inspect medical schools in England and France. These two years (1929-31) were filled to overflowing with new and marvelous sights, smells, sounds, and adventures. Along with his main purpose, to become acquainted with medical schools and professors, he was busy taking notes for his collections of essays and short stories. *Margarita . . .* was under preparation at the same time.

The publishing house, Zig-Zag, now one of the most important in Chile and hence in all South America, having projected a series of novels to be called *Colección de autores chilenos (Collection of Chilean Authors)*, chose *Margarita, el aviador y el médico* as the second of the collection.

MARGARITA, EL AVIADOR Y EL MEDICO

The story, although filled with breath-taking action, is relatively simple: Jorge Luna, a young pilot of the Chilean Air Force, escapes when other members of a conspiracy are captured, only because he has access to a plane that carries him over the Andes into Argentina. Margarita comes first in Luna's thoughts, for he realizes that their parting is probably forever. Luna overcomes many hardships to find his way, first to Buenos Aires and later to Europe. Margarita, feeling sure that her fiancé has been killed, tries to remake her life by plunging into a number of social, civic, and educational activities. She even attends classes in the School of Medicine where she meets the brilliant young doctor, Carlos Beytía.

Being convinced that Luna will never be able to return, Dr. Beytía and Margarita become engaged but when a letter arrives saying that Luna will come back if and when the revolution is successful, Beytía suggests to Margarita that they forget their love; Beytía does not want to be a traitor to his former friend and fellow conspirator. To try to forget Margarita, Beytía offers to have an affair with Adela Suárez, a conspirator who is under suspicion as a possible spy for the tyrant. His offer is accepted but Adela, a more experienced counter-spy, obtains from Beytía information that leads to a wholesale arrest of the revolutionaries. When Beytía is condemned to be executed, Adela, already romantically attached to him and conscience-striken because of her double dealings, asks the tyrant to commute his death sentence to a life-time exile on Rapa Nui, one of Chile's Easter Islands.

Margarita's parents, wishing to help their ill-fated daughter begin a new life, take her to Paris. One night when they are visiting a Parisian night club of low category they see Luna taking part in a very lascivious dance. When Margarita tries to induce him to leave this life, she is attacked by his dance partner, and, realizing that all is lost, she rushes out into the Parisian night.

> Her flight was without end . . .
> It was an endless, eternal flight.
> It was a flight from herself.[14]

Margarita . . . was quite well received having two editions soon after its appearance. It has, however, certain minor weaknesses that disappear in the author's more mature writings, *Paralelo 53 sur, Orestes y yo,* and *Viento negro.* But let us quote from two well known and experienced Chilean critics who read *Margarita* . . . without being able to see, until much later, these better and more mature works.

Hernán Díaz Arrieta (Alone), a very cautious and severe critic, wrote for *La Nación,* July 31, 1932:

> A critic, to tell the truth, ought not to criticize adversely any book unless he has not read it, that is to say, that he

had not been able to read it because of boredom. If he reaches the last page without skipping a period or comma, he is lost; he will have to praise. . . . Take note, then; we have read the entire novel by Juan Marin, entitled *Margarita, el aviador y el médico,* published by Zig-Zag and prologued by Hernán del Solar.[15]

Luis Durand, one of Chile's most important regional novelists and a profound student of his country's literature, wrote concerning *Margarita* . . . and its author:

> We hardly knew the author of this book. Once or twice we have talked with him briefly. Of course this has no importance in helping one form a judgment concerning his intellectual work. . . .
>
> We remember having read some of his book reviews; then we saw him at a meeting of the Writers Society . . . and once while eating in a down-town restaurant we heard him on the radio giving a lecture having to do with his profession. . . . This dynamic personality he is able to pass on to his characters in his writings. . . . *Margarita, el aviador y el médico* is a book full of attraction that tells the story of three lives with such a human accent as to make it very interesting.[16]

UN AVION VOLABA

(A Plane Was Flying)

This second novel by Juan Marin, much longer than his first, shows improvement in novelistic techniques, especially in character delineation and plot construction while keeping the same notable skills in description. It must be remembered that no person, either real or constructed by a creative writer, can be entirely consistent. Too much consistency makes for static characters. Therefore when the villain, Astorga, shows at last a consciousness of his evil deeds and in despair destroys himself with his plane, one does not find him for that reason a weaker character. The total length of this novel, 155 pages in the editions that we have examined and about fifty percent longer than

83

Margarita . . . , has given the novelist more space in which to demonstrate his improved techniques: more relevant descriptions, better developed characters, and improved plot.

The *Prologue* by Ernesto Montenegro deserves to be taken seriously, because those, who have had the pleasure of knowing Don Ernesto and of reading his criticisms, realize that he was an exceedingly restrained and honest workman. Especially penetrating and even prophetic are the few lines that we quote in English translation from this prologue:

> In the present novel the author gives us a sort of epitome of his many activities. He talks to us of aviation as a poet, and presents to us the airplane as a symbolic instrument thanks to which man can free himself from earthly miseries, broaden his vision of the world, and feel himself living with all of his potentialities under the stimulus of speed. In aviation he sums up humanity as it will be tomorrow.[17]

Dr. Marin begins this novel by introducing the three most important characters: Flight Instructor, Astorga; his favorite student, Jorge Garmendia; and the heroine and fiancée of the latter, Sonia. He uses skilfully three essential methods of creating characters: a) letting them talk, b) having others characterize them, and c) having them act in ways that will reinforce what has been said about them and what they themselves have said. Astorga is cruel, selfish, and bestial; Garmendia is idealistic, poetic, and altogether charming; Sonia is the perfect woman, understanding, friendly, and innocent—a one-man woman.

As the story opens, a bevy of young ladies is insisting on a flight in Astorga's plane, each one wanting to be first. Garmendia, whose respect for his flight instructor verges on adoration, insists that Sonia be given preference. Immediately Astorga shows his infatuation with Sonia but at the same time makes an attempt to frighten her with aerobatic maneuverings of his plane. Through his actions we learn how low Astorga will stoop to get his way with women. He is pictured as physically unattractive. Instead of compensating for this by developing spiritual attractions, he plans to get what he wants through trickery, deceit, and brute force.

Garmendia who has finished his instruction is chosen, partly at the instigation of Astorga who wants him out of the way, to fly with a group to Tierra del Fuego. Because of bad weather the flight is not very successful. Garmendia is forced to remain away from the vicinity of Santiago for several weeks. Astorga, feeling that he can force his attentions on Sonia, tricks her into being alone with him. He attacks her physically. Sonia, however, repels him. She is able to escape through a window but while wandering half-dazed through a field she falls in a river and allows herself to be drowned. Astorga, to protect himself, writes to Garmendia who is still far away in the South of Chile, telling him that Sonia has committed suicide because reports of Garmendia's affair with another have reached her.

On an expedition trying to find one of the lost planes, Garmendia has a serious accident, which, added to the tragedy of Sonia's death, causes him to become mentally unbalanced. When he is brought home, Garmendia's parents, already old and virtually helpless, turn over their son's care to the supervision of Astorga. We have a long description of the various treatments, including his seclusion in a sanatorium directed by a specialist in mental disorders.[18] Astorga's major concern is, of course, that Garmendia not recover because he might discover the truth and learn of the extent of Astorga's evil.

Garmendia finally dies. A military funeral is planned honoring the promising young aviator who had died in such tragic circumstances. During the funeral a number of planes were to fly around above the place of the funeral. Astorga is supposed to lead the group that will do a final dive over the cemetery. However, he continues the circling and finally, no longer able to calm his guilty conscience, sets his plane out to sea and is never seen again.

This last major work depending so heavily on aviation and medicine, in spite of bordering on the melodramatic, shows evidence of greatly improved novelistic techniques. The characters are more convincing, the conversation more natural, and the descriptions more relevant. Don Ernesto Montenegro, in his excellent prologue, once more provides us with some most discerning and concise judgments. We paraphrase again:

> As for novelistic skill, I shall only say that from the first lines of this novel, one finds presented the conflict in the opposing personalities of the characters and in the vigor of the dramatic incidents. The attention of the reader is awakened from the first moment as a tense cord that the strong hand pulls back never ceasing to control it.[19]

PARALELO 53 SUR

(Parallel 53 South)

We are now to discuss what is often called by many critics Juan Marin's masterpiece *Paralelo 53 sur (Parallel 53 South)*. The novelist had made liberal use of aviation in his first two novels, in many of his short stories, and in at least three of his best poems. This recurring reference to planes and flying is not surprising because his experiences in learning to pilot a plane were still recent enough to occupy his thoughts.

The extensive, provocative, and keen *Prologue* by Emilio Rodríguez Mendoza expresses exceptionally well what others have suggested, that Dr. Marin had continued writing poems, stories, and novels about aviation almost too long. He needed to get back to a new reality, to get his feet on the ground, so to speak. Evidently Rodríguez Mendoza had been following this young writer's career with more than a passing interest. We paraphrase a few lines:

> They told me that he (Juan Marin) was a big man wearing a sailor's cap over one eye, in love with propellers and steering wheels. He was looking for his literary niche.
> It has not always been easy for a writer to find it immediately. . . . I planned to ask him formally to leave the airplane in the snows of the Straits of Magellan and to begin at once to attack realism, because it is evident that

> anyone who has an imagination geared to the propeller
> of a plane will see life, whatever he focuses on, better than
> we mere earth-bound mortals.[20]

There is no doubt that Dr. Marin's writings, especially in the two novels *Viento negro* and *Paralelo* . . . , follow the more generally accepted realistic techniques, but his realism is not that of Flaubert, Zola, Pereda, or Blasco Ibáñez. Insofar as the two criteria so dear to Flaubert and Zola, careful observation and detailed description of places and attitudes, are concerned, we shall have to give Juan Marin a very high rating. Anyone who has seen the southern regions of Chile, even rapidly and superficially, recognizes the accuracy of his descriptions of places, attitudes, and happenings in *Paralelo*. . . . However, Dr. Marin's observation was automatic, unpremeditated, and not *ad hoc*. Even such a minor aspect of the realist's art as the judicious use of dialect becomes important in this novel.

Paralelo . . . , while going through various editions and several translations which help to prove its real artistic value, was criticized for its lack of unity and for the lack of a well-conceived character or two that would help carry the reader's interest through the seven or eight almost independent stories. We, however, agree with those who insist that the development of characters, important as it may be, is not indispensable to a great novel. Many times *Paralelo* . . . is compared to *La vorágine,* to *Los de abajo,* and to *Doña Bárbara,* novels that depend more heavily on environment than on character delineation. It is obvious that Dr. Marin could have made any one of the briefly presented characters of *Paralelo* . . . a hero or anti-hero by carrying him through the entire story. For example, what a hero Salvador Ponce could have been with only a slight increase in emphasis! Or even the repugnant, selfish, and ruthless José Alonso, a modern *pícaro,* would have made an excellent anti-hero! The question that probably occurred to Juan Marin is: "Would a hero or anti-hero, even while adding to the unity of the novel, have dimmed the picture of the environment?" At least he decided to leave his novel episodic and we are quite satisfied with this decision.

The author's synopsis, realistic and imaginative at the same time, is a very valuable aid to the casual reader; it gives us a glimpse of what we are to expect, ending with the invitation, and we paraphrase:

> We should prefer not to repeat what those four-hundred-year-old lips (i.e. lips of Magellan) would have said, but we invite the reader to guess what it would have been, reading these pages of pain, injustice, and of death.[21]

Paralelo 53 sur is made up of a series of episodes and pictures. Our first picture is of a settlement of Indians, Yaganes, who are overjoyed at the arrival of José Alonso, the trader who, with a horse and a mule laden with brandy, brightly colored cloth, etc., is coming to bargain for pelts of otter and seal. José Alonso has prospered but this is to be his last trip. He is becoming too old for the long, difficult ride over the mountains. Rosa, one of the Indian women, accepts the attentions of José Alonso during the night. Rosa's man, upset by these attentions, attempts to kill José Alonso but instead is killed by the two lovers.

Rosa and José Alonso realize that they will have to escape or be punished by the eye-for-an-eye justice of the Yaganes; they slip out in the midde of the night stealing many of the precious pelts. They reach Punta Arenas where we are introduced to the poverty and filth of one of the lower class boarding houses. José Alonso accepts a position as foreman of a large sheep ranch for which this part of Chile is famous.

Another character who becomes almost important enough to act as a unifying element in the novel is *el Chilote Grande* (The Big Man from Chiloé), a simple-minded giant of a man who has left his island home to seek greener pastures. When the *Chilote Grande* takes a position on the same ranch of which José Alonso is foreman, one begins to think that we are to have a typical novel of intrigue, for the *Chilote* has been looking on José Alonso's Indian woman with interest. But this naive giant whose friendship with Rosa provides him with information dangerous to José Alonso, information about certain underhanded and very profitable tactics carried on by the foreman, is eliminated by being locked up in one of the refrigeration plants used to preserve the carcasses of sheep.

Some of the seamy sides of life in Punta Arenas are shown. Salvador Ponce, a third possibility for the role of leading character, is introduced. Through his socialistic activities he has won the dislike of the criminal underworld. His near miraculous escape from drowning leaves him with one useless arm and a determination to be less open in his struggles to help the poor.

A visit to Punta Arenas during a bright week in late February or early March does not allow the tourist to see its squalor and poverty. Our visit to this metropolis on the Straits in 1952, more than fifteen years after the publication of *Paralelo* . . . , has provided us with a picture of a peaceful little city of brightly colored roof-tops looking out over the deep blue waters at low lying islands. It is quite possible that the impact of this novel may have called attention to conditions that existed earlier in that section, thus helping to improve them. We know that in 1952 slum clearance and urbanization (government housing projects) were progressing rapidly. Now a branch of the National University of Chile offers the young people of the region opportunities to begin their higher education. The possibilities of this region and its beauties are limitless. Many Chileans agree with the half-hidden thesis of Dr. Marin's novel, that the national government must give more attention to this very beautiful and promising southern tip of the republic.

The stories that form the skeleton of *Paralelo 53 sur,* in outline, are as follows:

José Alonso's visit to the Yaganes and his escape with Rosa; the sordid picture of Punta Arenas with the incident of the attempted drowning of Salvador Ponce and the introduction of the *Chilote Grande;* the trip of the little steamer *Olimpia* with the stop at the sheep ranch where José Alonzo is foreman, with the interpolation of the story of the death of the *Chilote Grande* in the refrigerator; the arrival of the gold-seekers and the attempt of some miners to molest the little girl Milka; the work of trying to salvage a wreck and the murder of the diver Manslave by Tarlton; the assignment of the expugilist as lighthouse keeper; the destruction of the oil well; and the rebellion on the sheep ranch.

There are only a few attempts to have some of the characters bind the semi-isolated events together. José Alonzo is present at the beginning and, although he disappears from the thread of the plot at times, he is back again at the end. It would have been relatively simple for Dr. Marin to maintain a greater unity through his characters but evidently he felt that *Paralelo* . . . was stronger with the milieu kept always very vivid before the reader.* The tragic weight of the environment is made and maintained central and all important. Merino Reyes says of this novel *"Paralelo . . . ,* a novel first published in 1936, . . . has been considered the outstanding production by Juan Marin. It is, at least, his most popular novel, one that shows him as a vigorous writer. . . ."[22]

EL SECRETO DEL DR. BALOUX

(Dr. Baloux's Secret)

This novel, one of the shorter ones, seventy-six pages, has a great deal of the fantastic and not a little of science fiction. The fantastic, however, is often fantasy only to those who will not accept a realism based primarily on psychic phenomena. Juan Marin early in his study of medicine became interested in psychology. In this tale we are introduced to Dr. Baloux who accepted the idea that human beings have three psychic states: the conscious, the subconscious, and the unconscious. Dr. Sigmund Freud, for whom Dr. Marin had always felt the greatest admiration, has studied these three states, trying to understand human

---

* We note, however, that almost automatically Dr. Marin gives personality to some of the characters of *Paralelo*. . . . Manuel Miranda Salloranzo says (See Bibliography D) ". . . al leer la novela tenemos el agrado de encontrar seres de carne y hueso, seres en que el pequeño detalle decidor nos muestra el individuo." (On reading the novel we are happy to find beings of flesh and blood, beings in which the little eloquent detail pictures for us the individual.)

actions and reactions. Dr. Marin had let his interest in the quirks of the human mind enter into other novels and short stories but in this one psychic matters become central.

Dr. Baloux had reached the conclusion that the unconscious can be isolated only after physical death occurs, and only for a very short time thereafter. By long experimentation he had developed, theoretically, the means of taking advantage of the short period immediately after death. He had discovered a metallic gas that would act to free the unconscious which could then express itself. His conclusion is that an interesting number of wonderful psychic discoveries may result from further experimentation. This novel is, then, a report on Dr. Baloux's experiments.

To test his theory, Dr. Baloux charters a boat, selects a number of semi-civilized Indians, and sets up his laboratory on an uninhabited island off the western coast of Chile. He takes along all of the materials he will need and asks that the boat return later in order to take his group back to the mainland.

Dr. Baloux decides to experiment on dogs, of which there were many on the island. The test works with the dogs; when immediately after physical death their unconscious is freed to express itself, they show their real feeling of hatred toward mankind. The question that still confronts the doctor is, "How can I experiment on human beings?" He knows that he cannot wilfully bring a person to death just to prove his theory. Finally, however, he discovers a young Indian boy whose death is imminent. This boy who has always been affectionate and docile shows, during the short unconscious period, open hatred toward his father, a hatred not too uncommon according to Freudian psychologists but unusual among the Indians who are trained from earliest childhood to respect, obey, and virtually worship their fathers.

Further questions arise: Will more civilized people show this same reaction during the unconscious period? Who will serve as guinea pigs? It seems that the always difficult step is to prove that sophisticated human beings, who have been conditioned through many generations to hide their deepest thoughts, will reveal their inmost feelings while unconscious.

The boat that is to take the group off the island returns but such a terrible storm strikes that it is driven high upon the rocks along the shore. The doctor's wife Sylvia and daughter Myriam have come with the rescue ship. As provisions are used up and all begin to die, the doctor has an inspiration. Why not use the famous metallic gas and experiment on his wife and daughter if and when all hope of saving them is gone? Dr. Baloux prepares everything, including his notebooks. His wife dies first; when she is given the metallic gas she reveals her innermost thoughts, some of them not at all flattering to her husband. The daughter comes next and she bares her secret thoughts and desires, showing that she is not the sweet, innocent girl that her father considered her to be. The doctor carefully registers these reactions. Almost without realizing it he has inhaled enough of the gas to go through the same experience. He continues to write in his notebook, including hitherto well-guarded secrets, up to the very moment of his death.

Finally a second rescue ship comes. The notebook is found and it serves as the basis for *El secreto.* . . . This short novel, an excellent example of Dr. Marin's science fiction writing, has remained quite popular. It again demonstrates his interest in the workings of the human mind.

NAUFRAGIO

(Shipwreck)

Naufragio, also a very short novel, has its inception on the wreck of the *Birkdale* but much imaginative element is present. It is quite possible that the author had considered a longer work, for we find such hints as "deseo abreviar" (I wish to be brief) and "no he de contar los mil y un detalles . . ." (I am not going to tell the thousand and one details). The background of the narrator Roca is given in resumé. He is a graduate engineer from the University of San Felipe in Santiago. He is near starvation in England (where he has been stranded) when he is finally accepted by Captain Schwarz, master of a sailing boat, the *Birkdale,* that is leaving England for Callao, Peru. Roca, in spite of his superior education, will be working as a common sailor living with the crew in the dark, crowded quarters before the mast.

The first three months on board are uneventful; the ship reaches the neighborhood of Cape Horn before bad weather begins. As they sail around the Horn, a serious storm develops and, what is more tragic, the coal with which the ship is loaded starts to burn. This is attributed to spontaneous combustion but a negro deck-hand talks about the ghost of a man who was suffocated in the hold. He considers this ghost responsible for the fire; they round the Cape successfully but are unable to extinguish the conflagration. To protect the two lifeboats from the blaze, the captain has them lowered, manned, and pulled along behind the ship. Eventually the crews of these two boats, feeling that they can reach shore safely, cut themselves loose. Boats and crews are never heard from again.

The *Birkdale* is finally wrecked on a small, rocky, uninhabited island. The only food is an edible sea-weed and a few shell-fish that can be found on the small beach among the rocks. Captain Schwarz, realizing the hopelessness of the situation, decides to take the dinghy and two companions to go in search of help. This leaves eleven men on the island living in a small tent that they have set up, with practically no food and little hope of seeing their captain again. After a few days they begin to show signs of insanity. The men have nightmares, imagine they see rescue ships, become easily irritated, and even break into unrestrainable fits of shouting and running about the island.

The food becomes more and more difficult to find so that little by little cannibalism is hinted. It is decided that the Peruvian boy will be sacrificed, but no one wants to be guilty of murdering him. He is ordered to sleep outside in the hope that he will die of the cold. Roca is, at first, against this cannibalism but eventually accepts the idea. Manuel, the Peruvian boy, does not die from exposure. One morning he begins to shout, "The captain has come back! Look at the steamer's smoke! Captain

Schwarz has brought help!"[23] Although the men are glad that the captain has come to their rescue, they seem to be sorry that they did not have the experience of cannibalism.

There are some fantastic elements used from time to time in *Naufragio*. One episode concerns the famous legend that exists among sailors throughout the world—the ghost ship. One night the eleven shipwrecked men see on the horizon a brightly lighted, full-rigged ship going north. They can see nobody on board but they hear voices and songs coming from the vessel. Moving with incredible speed, it sails directly toward them finally passing over their heads. This is the "Galeuche," the celebrated pirates' ship with the souls of all the dead mariners aboard. According to the legend, this ship is often seen on clear nights by sailors who are traveling near the coast. We have already mentioned the belief of the negro sailor that the soul of a man suffocated in the hold is bringing them their bad luck. Another item that may be considered additional evidence of the novelist's interest in the occult is a recurring, fantastic dream of Roca, our raconteur.

It is interesting to read from Juan Marin's *Prólogo (Prologue)* that the story has much authentic material taken from the report of the wreck of a ship named the *Birkdale* near the Nelson Straits. We paraphrase the ending of Dr. Marin's *Prólogo:*

> I dedicate to all the men of the sea of my country, who constantly risk their lives in the southern seas, this story half real, half fantastic, as life itself.[24]

ORESTES Y YO

(Orestes and I)

Dr. Marin's interest in psychology and psychic phenomena can be seen in many of his stories and in his novel *Un avión volaba*. Sooner or later he would feel impelled to write a novel based primarily on the workings of the human mind. *Orestes y yo* may be considered a very carefully planned and executed study of abnormal psychology not only in the main character but in the three members of the family of Dr. Fraga.

Orestes y yo recalls our youthful readings and enjoyment of some of the novels of Dickens that speak of boarding schools: *David Copperfield, Oliver Twist,* and others. We are sure that Dr. Marin, an omnivorous reader, had also read them and had, in a very tenuous way, based some of his attitudes toward boarding school scenes on Dickens' writings. The great difference is that Dickens was not a trained psychologist and had not had the advantage of reading Freud. Dr. Marin seems to be following a well thought out plan in *Orestes y yo* for it is well organized.[25]

Because this novel is based on mental aberrations, there is a minimum of external action. The real conflict, and hence the important part of the story, begins when Dr. Fraga makes the acquaintance of Teresa. She is a moody, enigmatic, artistic girl who at her best could be the life of the party. From the beginning we see that Dr. Fraga is more interested in himself than in Teresa. His attitude, probably, is based on an inferiority complex; he worries not so much about his love for her as about her love for him. Even in the story of Fraga as a boy in Constitución, certain characteristics of the self-centered individual are brought out.

This self-doubt is shown by a description of Fraga's actions during the wedding, a simple church affair. Fraga decides to discover, in a peculiar way, whether Teresa really loves him. By arriving late at the church he hopes, no doubt, that he will find Teresa worried, maybe in despair. She, however, is the calmest person in the wedding party and does not even question Fraga about his tardiness.

Toward the end of their European honeymoon, Teresa announces that she is going to have a child and that she wants to return to Chile as soon as possible. At first Fraga is happy but almost immediately begins to show jealousy; he even suggests that it might be well to interrupt the pregnancy. Teresa's answer shows us in advance the future conflict. "No! You do not know what this child means to me!" In due time a boy, to whom Fraga insists the name Orestes be given, is born without complications. Almost from the beginning Teresa gives all of her attention to

Orestes, neglecting her husband who is already suspecting this mother-son fixation.

It is well to remember that *Orestes* . . . is based on a supposed diary that Dr. Fraga had turned over to the narrator in Switzerland. The doctor, who is a trained psychiatrist, hints at mental aberrations in Teresa and as soon as Orestes starts to develop, he also is pronounced by the father to be affected by abnormal mental tendencies. Perhaps not knowing exactly why, Fraga wants to send Orestes to private boarding schools, and even to a sanatorium. Teresa refuses to talk about this, insisting on the perfect normality of their son.

The spiritual as well as the physical separation of Teresa and Dr. Fraga becomes greater and greater until finally he moves out of their home, with the excuse that he needs to be nearer his work in the hospital. In his diary he expresses the fear that Teresa may try to poison him. The association between mother and son continues to be very close. We can see that Fraga fears a spiritual incestuous relationship.

Orestes becomes ill but Fraga will not call in an outside doctor, saying that the illness is not serious and that he can take care of it. When Teresa finally decides on her own authority to call in a specialist, it is too late. Orestes dies! In her grief Teresa accuses her husband of intentionally neglecting their son. Although at first he angrily denies it, he eventually confesses that he had hoped to save their marriage by allowing Orestes to die. In the play based on this novel, Dr. Marin makes this conflict clearer; he gives Orestes more personality and a much stronger role. Before Teresa can have Fraga put in a sanatorium for the criminally insane, he escapes to Switzerland. As mentioned previously, it was in Switzerland that the author was given the diary from which the novel was developed.

Orestes y yo is one of the most interesting novels of its kind that we have ever read. As is usual with Juan Marin, there are descriptions that verge on the poetic, characters that are well constructed, and the same carefully written prose. It is never a simple task to create real-life characters in novels, and when the novel deals primarily with mental quirks, as in the personalities of Teresa and Dr. Fraga, the matter becomes even more complicated.

VIENTO NEGRO

(Black Wind)

Viento negro is frankly sociological and in many ways Juan Marin's best novel: better planned, better unified, and with more carefully delineated characters. We have discussed the lack of unity in *Paralelo 53 sur,* agreeing that unity of plot, usually of prime importance, must sometimes be sacrificed for others, for example that of environment. In *Viento negro* environment is not neglected but is designed primarily to reinforce the realism of the action. Although Dr. Marin's prose fiction is filled with poetic descriptions, few surpass those we have here of the following: little Daisy, the blue-eyed daughter of the English director and of the beautiful park of Puerto Amargo. These two semi-poetic visions of loveliness are cancelled by the portrayal of the squalor of the *conventillos*[26] and the filth of the harbor seen by the crews of the Chilean fleet anchored in semicircle in the bay. Side by side exist in *Viento negro* great beauty and unspeakable ugliness. We can only guess that the presentation of these two extremes was carefully planned by Juan Marin who doubtlessly had noted this technique in the novels of Victor Hugo. In this story the elegant park, the beautiful chalets occupied by the capitalists, and the modishly dressed and carefully protected Daisy contrast sharply with the way of life of the miners and stevedores. There are no didactic interpolations needed to point out to the reader these social injustices. The facts, the events, and the characters are allowed to speak for themselves as the great theorists of realism have always demanded.

We find emphasized in *Viento negro* the use of the picturesque Spanish of the under-privileged Chilean day laborers, the special macaronic speech of the Italian owners of the *boliche,* and the ungrammatical, infinitive-laden Spanish of Mr. Sanders, the English overseer. Previously Dr. Marin had made some use of various dialects to increase the illusion of reality, but here he has carried this technique to greater and more artistic extremes.

As for characters, Juan Marin has given us in *Viento negro* several interesting and superbly developed ones: Perico, the hero, the poor boy who rises above his environment to modest success; Perico's mother, not perfect except in her maternal love, a love that will allow her to accept anything, even prostitution, to feed her family; Perico's father "El Pelado" (Baldy), the hard-working, sober, family-loving man, pictured briefly, and eliminated in the first chapter; "el Gigante" (Giant), a strong, simple, single-minded, brave man who is a second father (god-father) to Perico; Nancy, the "innocent" prostitute whose frustrated motherhood almost finds satisfaction as she tries to give Perico what he needs; the villain "el Lagarto" (The Lizard), tricky, cruel, envious, a real twenty-four carat scoundrel; the Italian owner of the "boliche" (drink shop of low category) and his buxom wife, both of whom in spite of their poverty and lack of education, show extraordinary kindness toward Perico. Even the minor characters, for example Daisy, the attractive little daughter of Perico's boss, are well introduced with a few significant phrases.

The story is relatively simple. We note the similarity of the first chapter of this novel to the story "Puerto negro" already discussed, but in the novel Perico's father, "el Pelado" (Baldy), is suffocated in the bunkers of a ship coaling up in the harbor. The compensation for Baldy's death is soon spent leaving the family in dire financial straits. Perico's god-father, "el Gigante" (The Giant), helps the boy obtain work with the overseer of the English company in charge of the coaling operations. This is not sufficient and so Perico's mother rents her bed, the one she has been sharing with him, to first one and afterwards to two miners who occupy it in turn. Both men insist that the "services" of their landlady are included with the price of the bed. When Perico learns that his mother has become a quasi-prostitute, he leaves home and is allowed to use a back room in the *boliche* paying for his bed and odds and ends of food by waiting on tables. When "el Lagarto" calls Perico's mother a *puta* (prostitute) the boy strikes him with a heavy bottle. Although "el Gigante" has promised to protect the boy, "el Lagarto" slips into the *conventillo,* severely wounds the boy and kills the mother who is trying to shield her son. After a long period of hospitalization Perico recovers enough to be given a place on a Chilean naval vessel as a cabin boy. Thus Part I ends.

As Part II begins we find that through intelligence and hard work Perico has earned an appointment to signal officer's school. This means that if all goes well he will eventually become a naval officer. The fleet, including Perico's ship, is ordered to return to Puerto Amargo to aid the city during a strike of stevedores. He is thus forced to take sides against his former friends and, in his attempts to make peace between the strikers and the naval authorities, he is accused by both sides of being a traitor.

In the meantime Perico looks up his brothers and a sister who has been working as an errand girl in a brothel. When the *madame* of the brothel learns that Perico plans to take his sister away from her questionable surroundings, the *madame* turns the twelve-year-old errand girl over to three rough men. Here, as in several other stories, Dr. Marin shows his sympathy for women who for one reason or another are forced into a life of prostitution. Just when it appears that Perico is going to be able to make peace between the laborers and the ship owners, he is drowned as he is trying to swim ashore to make a last effort to settle the strike.

Again we should like to say of *Viento* . . . that we consider it the novelistic climax, the most mature of Dr. Marin's novels, as well as one of the best Chilean novels dealing with the problems of the lower classes. Because of the several well-sketched characters, the interesting action, and the author's skill in presenting the environment, one's interest never flags.

It is important to note that Juan Marin said that this was the second title of a planned trilogy. We paraphrase:

"Thus as *Paralelo* . . . tried to capture one aspect of our unknown country, *Viento* . . . tried to make known another. Later if Destiny allows it, there will appear *Desierto fecundo (Desert Wealth)*, with which the trilogy we had proposed will be completed."[27]

It is our opinion that *Viento* . . . shows that Dr. Marin had finally found himself, that it is after all as a novelist, a realistic, socialistic novelist, the voice of the under dog, that he is to be remembered. Had he been allowed the time to finish his planned *Desierto fecundo* and possibly others depicting problems of his beloved Chile, all written in the fullness of his creative powers and enriched by his omnivorous reading and extraordinary experiences, even greater literary treasures would have eventuated.[28]

MUERTE EN SHANGHAI

(Death in Shanghai)

This short novel was published in Spain soon after Juan Marin's resignation from the Chilean diplomatic corps had been accepted by President Carlos Ibáñez in 1952. Although we do not feel that *Muerte* . . . adds greatly to Marin's reputation, it shows again his great versatility. Had he been interested in writing as a means of making his fortune, he could have produced scores of novels of international intrigue, because his experiences in this field were exceptionally rich.

It is the story of a Chinese quisling, Fu Chi-cheng. Yo Chang-ló, member of *The Blue Shirts,* an organization dedicated to the task of fighting collaborationists, is given the assignment of eliminating Fu Chi-cheng, figure-head mayor of the city of Shanghai. His task must be carried out alone. He is able to discover that the quisling mayor has many houses in Shanghai but he frequents one in the center of the city in order to be with his latest and very attractive Manchu concubine, Lin-Er. The executioner-to-be arranges to be appointed chief cook in this house.

With the assistance of Lin-Er (who soon lets him know that she hates Fu Chi-cheng) and an old lady who looks after her,

Yo Chang-ló manages to dope most of the guards and to kill the mayor in his bed. He then escapes to a Buddhist monastery where the novelist has found the manuscript from which *Muerte en Shanghai* is developed.

Although this is primarily a romantic, melodramatic novel of intrigue, enough description, place-names, and references to Chinese customs are present to give it a touch of realism. Dr. Marin had written several books that show his interest in and love for China and the real Chinese people, but one sees here, also, his dislike for double dealing or treachery of any sort.

There is some love element in the novel but it is kept well under control; love must not interfere with one's patriotic duties. We are introduced to Mei-Ling, a fellow member of *The Blue Shirts,* for whom Yo Chang-ló appears to have a deep affection. But his love for her and a later love awakened in him for the Mayor's concubine, Lin-Er, are not allowed to take first place in his thoughts.

Muerte . . . , of less than one hundred pages, was published by the Spanish Editorial Rollán in 1953. Other leading writers included in the same series, *Novelistas de hoy* (Contemporary Novelists), are Pío Baroja, Carmen Laforet, José Cela, and Alberto Insúa.

General Remarks Concerning Prose Fiction

In discussions of Juan Marin as a writer of prose fiction, we have found ourselves pointing to his novels as the climax to this type of literary production. In an earlier chapter we have written about his poetry and eventually we shall say something about his essays, his philosophical writings, and his travel books. We shall, however, for the present consider him primarily as a novelist. One always realizes that such a statement is a bit presumptive, that with the passing of time well-documented critics may give first place to his poems, to his books on medical subjects, his philosophical writings, or his travel books. All have merited high praise but for the moment we prefer the novels and of the novels

Viento negro. We make this statement in spite of the fact that first place is almost universally given to *Paralelo 53 sur.*

In the blurb in the front pages of the Zig-Zag edition of *Viento negro,* published in 1960, we read paraphrased in English:

> Nevertheless, the most valuable contribution of Dr. Marin's writing is in his novels, among which it suffices to name: *The Death of Julian Aranda, A Plane Was Flying,* and *Death in Shanghai.*[29]

What many consider the most complete, the most thoughtful, and the most judicious criticism of Dr. Marin's prose fiction is an article by Luis Merino Reyes published in *Inter-American Review of Bibliography.* He has insisted on the fallacy of attempting to classify writers as realistic or imaginative. No realism can nor ought to be pure; it is the imagination, especially in Juan Marin's prose fiction, that is most important. This is true even in those novels like *Viento negro* that come very near to the realistic techniques so dear to Zola and Maupassant. We paraphrase briefly in English and invite the interested reader to enjoy the original in our *General Notes* to this chapter.

> And after naming other authors, we say that Juan Marin had read carefully Joseph Conrad, Blaise Cendrars whom he translated, Somerset Maugham . . . and also, as we have noted, Guillaume Apollinaire, the prose writer. . . . Only the imagination in Marin was maintained faithful to a certain metaphysical undercurrent . . . which is paradoxical considering his medical background and training. . . .[30]

Merino Reyes also quotes generously from "El hombre de música," often classifed as one of Juan Marin's better fantastic stories:

> He rapidly lost the notion of reality and entered the enchanted world of dreams.[31]

Merino Reyes continues:

> Once we heard a phenomenal Chilean writer, who was talking about himself, (speak) of the importance of imag-

> inative literature. . . . We thought then as now that, in
> that literary latitude, Juan Marín has been misunderstood
> and, for that reason, forgotten. The majority of his stories
> and the climax of his novels, for example *Viento negro,*
> have an imaginative accent; the sudden change from a
> monotonous and oppressive realism is induced perhaps by
> the author's life of constant movement and his feeling that
> literature is fictional, made possible within certain limits,
> but always extraordinary. This imaginative force is harmo-
> nized as much with what the characters say as with what
> they do. . . .[32]

Merino Reyes agrees with the opinion of the majority of critics,
that Juan Marín's masterpiece is *Paralelo 53 sur.* After discussing
the episodic construction and lamenting the fact that such super
characters as Salvador Ponce are condemned to minor roles, he
accepts as sound the novelist's decision to leave the work episodic.

In his critical opinion Merino Reyes has summed up exceedingly well in an excellent and comprehensive appreciation of the
important and essential elements that give to Juan Marín's maturer
fiction its lasting values. We paraphrase a few excerpts and quote
the entire paragraph in our *General Notes:*

> And we continue, without being able to finish (to our
> satisfaction) these few lines, seduced by the artistic treasure
> of Juan Marín. . . . Juan Marín belongs to those human
> values able to maintain carefully a certain agreement be-
> tween ends and means. The destiny of Juan Marín was to
> write novels, short stories, essays; to make cultures known;
> to defend, as a part of this destiny: liberality of thought,
> decency, and self-respect of mankind. His means (i.e. ways
> in which he reached his destiny or ends) consisted of life
> far removed from his country, extended to the farthest
> reaches of the world. . . . But those superior men who
> have lived at our side, that have lived within reach of our
> hands, make us believe in dreams of glory and immortal-
> ity.[33]

From time to time we have called attention to our author's
deviation from realism, his determination to make use of his
imagination, of the fantastic, including the use of extrasensory

perception, telepathy, and intuition. Professor Anderson Imbert recognizes this in Juan Marin and others of the same generation:

> Some authors escape from reality by use of the ocean, adventure, dreams, and pseudo-scientific fantasy, . . .
>
> Although Juan Marin is the author, among many other books, of a description of the life of suffering in the vicinity of the Straits of Magellan, he has also a dimension of the fantastic, as one can see in his *Cuentos de viento y agua*.[34]

Hundreds of pages of criticism have been written concerning Dr. Marin's literary production, especially about his prose fiction; we hope that from these we have chosen the most significant. This section cannot be ended without making brief citations from Dr. José Balseiro's excellent study. His criticism has to do primarily with two of Juan Marin's novels, *Paralelo* . . . and *Viento negro*. (See also an interesting study of *Paralelo* . . . in *El Mercurio de Santiago,* December 19, 1965; See our note 35.) Dr. Balseiro analyzes carefully each of these two novels from the point of view of: character construction, description, and action. Without making specific reference to the episodic nature of *Paralelo* . . . , this critic evidently accepts it as legitimate. We paraphrase a few lines here and give a generous quotation in our *General Notes* in Dr. Balseiro's own Spanish:

> The number of episodes (cuadros) of perversity, with no place allowed for optimism, and the shadows that invariably smother with their evil waves the souls that pass through them, never seem to us conventional or invented fabrications of the novelist. . . . This (novelist) was able to paint . . . pictures of unforgettable and constant value not subjected to political or legalistic controls.

Again Dr. Balseiro says directing his remarks to *Viento negro:*

> In both works (*Paralelo* . . . and *Viento negro*) we see made evident the author's interest in the sociological problems of the proletariat and of *the little people.* . . . The events occur so smoothly and vividly in *Viento negro* that we follow them as though we were eye witnesses. . . . Although the characters and their language are frankly

> Chilean, their sentiments are universal. . . . Juan Marin's
> affection for the Chilean navy is evident.[35]

As a critic of recognized honesty and undoubted penetration, Dr. Balseiro could not refrain from pointing out what he (and we agree with him) thought to be a weakness in *Paralelo*. . . . He felt that the final episode relating to the conflict between the foreign and native engineers, insofar as the oil wells were concerned, could have been eliminated without loss to the artistry, maybe even leaving the novel all the stronger.

> . . . Everything is developed with the legitimate breath
> of truth. Never-the-less, one would have to make exceptions
> to the last chapter. In this chapter, so it seems to us, the
> Chilean in Juan Marin has won out over the writer.[36]

SECTION IV

TWO PLAYS

It would have been most unusual had Juan Marin not experimented with dramatic literature. This often has a special appeal to all and, normally, a young writer spends some time at dramatic composition. Some of those who have tried to write plays, in some cases successfully, have later become top flight novelists. Dr. Marin undertook his two plays, two that have merited printed editions, while he was still relatively young in years but old in literary experience. He probably did not seriously consider a new career as a writer of drama. We shall discuss quite briefly his dramatic compositions *Orestes y yo* and *El emperador Kwang Hsü*. They were published in Spanish and English in Tokyo, *Ediciones "Asia-América,"* 1940 and 1941 respectively.[37]

ORESTES Y YO[38]

This play is based on the novel of the same title (discussed earlier in this chapter) with only minor changes. The converting of a relatively long novel to a three act play offers many possibilities and presents certain problems. The dramatic version may attempt to cover all of the material first used in the novel or it may, as in the case of *Look Homeward Angel* based on Thomas Wolfe's very long novel, choose certain limited parts disregarding the more slowly moving action of the prose fiction. Juan Marin has chosen to represent on the stage three of the most dramatic sections of the novel, to introduce some action not occurring in it, and to have a few other events that the author deemed important reported by various characters. He has been well advised to give Orestes more personality, a greater chance to speak for himself in the drama than in the novel, because this sharpens his individuality. Also Teresa's image becomes much stronger in the play. By concentrating Dr. Fraga's life into a much shorter period, Dr. Marin pictures him more vividly than in the novel.

In the first act two very well drawn characters are emphasized, one of Dr. Fraga's former companions in the medical school, Dr. Barcia, and his wife Julia. The humor of these two is in sharp contrast to the tragic trend of the play and the seriousness of the other personages. They do everything possible to smooth over the points of disagreement between Dr. Fraga and his wife—the most important being Teresa's fixation for her son Orestes.

The first act opens with an orchestra practice session; Teresa has been discovered to be a highly trained pianist who is to help with the orchestra. She is the center of interest, for people remember her as the woman who took part so heroically in a student uprising. The police are still looking for her, the enigmatic young lady who defied them at the risk of her life. Dr. Fraga, who is present at the rehearsal, becomes for the first time in his life interested in a woman—Teresa. The first act ends with Dr. Fraga exclaiming the one word, "Woman!"

The second act opens thirteen years later. Orestes, the son of Dr. Fraga and Teresa, is now twelve years old. In the first scene Teresa is playing the piano while Orestes, enchanted, listens to the music and watches fascinated by the graceful, rapid movement of her hands as she executes skilfully and artistically the most difficult compositions. The special relationship between mother and son is quite apparent. Dr. Fraga feels abandoned by his wife and tries in several ways to separate them. One possibility that comes to his mind is to send his son to a boarding school. Orestes is frightened by the idea of being parted from his mother, and Teresa refuses to consider sending her son away. In the midst of this dispute, Dr. Calzada, a long time friend of the family, enters and begins to question some of the far-out ideas of Dr. Fraga. This discussion becomes so bitter that Fraga orders Dr. Calzada to leave.

In act three, a few years later, we find Orestes in bed with a fever that his father has diagnosed as "something of little importance." But Teresa, suspecting it to be more serious, calls in Dr. Calzada who after examining the boy reports that he is dying. After Orestes' death, Teresa, in her terrible grief, accuses her husband of neglecting his son, of allowing him to die. At first Dr. Fraga denies this but finally, now almost insane, he confesses that he has indeed allowed Orestes to die, but that it was in order to try to save his marriage. The play ends as Dr. Fraga shouts:

> In my head there are fighting the forces which move the
> world: love and hatred, beauty and crime, life and death;
> and only I am the judge, and I only am the judge (shouting
> more loudly) AND I ONLY AM THE JUDGE.[39]

It is difficult to determine whether Dr. Marin planned a staging of *Orestes y yo*. We know that this was written during one of the busiest periods of his career and that he would have found it almost impossible to leave other important work that he was doing to give his personal attention to supervising the staging of a play, which usually means some revision and at times rewriting. We believe that with the right kind of direction and a sympathetic audience it could have been a very successful dramatic production.

EL EMPERADOR KWANG-HSU[40]

This drama was rightly given the subtitle of *Adaptación histórica* (Historical Adaptation). It is quite evident that *El emperador . . .* was not intended for staging; it is an *Arm Chair*

Play that could easily be made into a film. The action covers several years immediately before the Chinese Republic under Dr. Sun Yat-Sen came into existence. Juan Marin adds very little to the historical facts, only enough to increase one's interest. There are some twenty characters, twelve of whom are fairly important to the plot.

We have repeatedly mentioned Dr. Marin's intellectual curiosity; he had gone to great efforts to document himself on the history, geography, and politics of China as we shall see later when we discuss his books on China, especially *El alma de China* and *Mesa de mah-jong*. He appends a short bibliography which will help the curious to understand the play better.

The central theme of *El emperador* . . . is a woman's thirst for power and her determination to retain this power in spite of the new emperor's just claims to the political control of China. This woman, the Dowager Empress Tzú-Hsi, was a concubine of the former emperor and the only one of his wives or concubines to give him a son. The son was made emperor when his father died, but the Dowager managed to be the real authority simply by seeing that he had opportunities to lose the respect of his people because of his drinking, gluttony, and debauchery. Although she could not officially be the ruler, the Dowager hoped to continue governing by placing her grandson, Kwang Hsü, on the throne. She found him a consort, Lung Yu, who quite willingly acted as a spy keeping the Dowager fully informed about Kwang Hsü's every act and thought. The most appealing character of the entire play is Perla, a concubine who demonstrates a selfless affection for Kwang Hsü and an interest in his ambitions to become a real emperor and to institute much needed reforms in the government.

The story of the play act by act will be helpful. In Act I Kwang Hsü is beginning to make his plans to act on his own authority, his central idea being to modernize China, to point her toward the Occident, to improve her army and navy, and to send thousands of the most promising young people to study in the great universities of the world. But at the end of Act I, when confronted by the Dowager, he lacks the courage to carry out his plans. The act ends with Kwang Hsü saying to Perla, his favorite concubine: "She is more powerful; she is stronger."

In Act II, while the young emperor is conferring with his advisers, Perla asks permission to bring in a holy man, a Taoist monk, who has an important message that he has traveled months and hundreds of miles to give to the emperor. The message foretells the temporary triumph of the Dowager and the defeat of the Chinese armies by the foreigners. Kwang Hsü, however, is determined to go ahead with his plans to modernize China. But one of his generals helped by Kwang Hsü's consort, Lung Yu, exposes these plans to the Dowager, who has the young emperor made prisoner and declared incapable of governing. Perla, the young concubine, is executed off stage by being thrown in a well. The Chinese armies have been defeated, as prophesied by the holy man, the Taoist monk. The court flees from Peking.

Act III takes place ten years later. The Dowager is still regent, but knowing that she has but a short time to live, she appoints her successor and orders Kwang Hsü to take his life by drinking a poison. The act ends as General-President Dr. Sun Yat-Sen enters to pronounce the peroration: "The dynasty has died. . . . But China has only been sleeping! Let us awaken her! China will live! China is eternal!"[41]

We repeat that these two plays were probably not written to be staged. With proper directing and minor changes *Orestes y yo* would be very interesting and effective. *El emperador* . . . could easily be converted into a scenario for a documentary, historical film and it might be successfully presented by the Chinese Classical Theater. To help make *Orestes* . . . more appealing on the stage only minor changes would be needed, for there are already present some very dramatic situations. The orchestra practice session, although off-stage, could contribute much by having the musicians enter through the stage, carrying their instruments, and discussing a new symphony scheduled to begin rehearsals.

Also, instead of having Teresa's part in a student uprising reported, she could come on stage out-of-breath as though fleeing the police who are in hot pursuit. The conversation between the police and the on-stage characters as the latter ingeniously mislead the officers of the law, could offer humor and suspense. Even more could be made of Dr. Fraga's awakening of interest in Teresa, the first woman to arouse his love. Although the lapse of time between the first and second acts cannot be eliminated, the time, otherwise, might be condensed.

As for *El emperador* . . . , much could be made of the costuming: the glittering trappings of the last days of the Chinese Empire, the drab clothing of the Taoist monk, the more modern clothing of Kwang Hsü, and the much braided uniform of President-General Sun Yat-Sen. The contrast in the personalities of the four main characters—the Dowager Empress, forceful, almost masculine; Kwang Hsü's legitimate consort, Lung Lu, underhanded and deceitful; Perla, the self-effacing, loyal concubine; and Kwang Hsü, idealistic, poetic, and weak-willed—could be emphasized even more. Because of the total disregard of the unities of time and place, this would more easily be converted to a film, but it has some possibilities as a staged play.

CHAPTER IV

Philosophies, Religions, and Civilization

In this chapter[1] we shall discuss Juan Marin's writings which
have as their main purpose the understanding of the Far East:
China, Tibet, and India. These books are: *El Tibet misterioso y
sus lamas (Mysterious Tibet and Her Lamas); China: Lao-Tszé,
Confucio y Buda (China: Lao-Tszé, Confucius, and Buddha);
El alma de China (The Soul of China);* and *Mesa de mah-jong
(The Mah-jong Table).* The first three books were written during those months of 1943 while the Marins were confined in
the Chilean legation in Shanghai, a city which was at that time
under the Japanese occupation. *China* was first published in
1944 in a beautiful edition with illustrations in the *Colección
Grandes Obras Actuales* by Espasa Calpe, Argentina. This edition
was soon out of print and because of difficulties of securing the
proper grade of paper to duplicate the first edition, Espasa Calpe
brought out a paper-back printing in three separate volumes:
*Lao-Tszé o el universalismo mágico, Confucio o el humanismo
didactizante,* and *Buda o la negación del mundo* in the *Colección
Austral.* We shall discuss *China,* therefore, as three separate publications using the *Colección Austral.* But first we analyze briefly
El Tibet misterioso y sus lamas.

EL TIBET MISTERIOSO Y SUS LAMAS

(Mysterious Tibet and Her Lamas)[2]

This essay was published separately from *China,* as Juan
Marin explains in his *Introducción* which he calls *Preliminar,*
because Buddhism took on different aspects in Tibet and Mon-
golia than in other Far Eastern countries. As is almost always
the case when a new religious belief is introduced into a country,

previous religions cannot be eradicated entirely. Shamanism and Bompoism, a mixture of polytheism and demonology, had an influence on Buddhism when it arrived.

The historical arrival of Buddhism is outlined by Dr. Marin:

I. A Tibetan monarch, Srongtan Gangpó, in the year 641 A.D., married one of the daughters of the Emperor of China. She brought to Tibet her belief in Buddhism and a small statue of this great religious leader.

II. A Buddhist missionary, Padma Sambhava, arrived about a century later from India and by accepting certain practices and credos of the original religions was able to set up the Lamaistic Buddhism which Dr. Marin discusses in *El Tibet misterioso y sus lamas*.

III. Kublai Khan gave his official approval of Lamaism in Tibet in the thirteenth century although he recognized that it was inferior to the Buddhism followed in the rest of China.

IV. In 1417 a Chinese religious reformer, Tsong-Khapá, came to Tibet to spend his life trying to purify Lamaism, establishing the "Yellow Church," though the "Red Church" continued to exist.

As was to be expected, Dr. Marin emphasizes the cultural side of Lamaism. The famous temple-fortress at Lhassa, the Potala, with its beautiful setting, was at the same time the center of both the political and religious powers. The Dalai Lama lived in the Potala. Some sort of tribute by every phase of civil as well as religious life had to be paid to the priestly class, which became more and more powerful.

It is, however, to the poet-mystic, Milarespa, that our author gives most attention. Milarespa was considered almost an idiot when a boy, and his parents encouraged him to live a life of crime. One of the religious leaders seemed to have sensed at once that there was something unusual in this idiot-criminal and with patience was able, gradually, to show his disciple the great lessons of Buddhism at its best. Milarespa eventually had a following of his own, but it is in the poetical presentation of his religious feelings that we find his major contribution.[3] Dr. Marin has translated from French, Milarespa's poem, calling our attention to the purity and spirituality of it. We paraphrase part of the poem in English giving more generous quotations in Dr. Marin's Spanish in our *General Notes:*

> Rétchungpá, you who resemble my heart,
> Listen to this song, full of precepts that embody my last will.
> In the ocean of transmigration of the three worlds
> The body with its apparent reality is the great sinner.
>
> . . . . .
>
> As long as we worry about food and clothing
> There is no denial of the world.
> Oh!, renounce the world, Rétchungpá!
>
> . . . . .
>
> Contemplation, meditation and ecstasy,
> Accustom yourself to think of
> This life, the next, and the Limbos
> As a single thing.
>
> . . . . .
>
> This is my final teaching!
> This is the end of my will:
> Afterwards nothing exists, Oh, Rétchungpá![4]
>
> . . . . .
>
> *Note how pure is the Buddhist doctrine (expressed here)*
> *in spite of its having been composed by an unorthodox*
> *Tibetan. The most orthodox 'hinayanist' would not have ex-*
> *pressed it in a more perfect manner. (Note by Juan Marin.)*[5]

Marin makes reference to certain Tibetan drama, insisting on the fact that, in spite of its resemblance to Chinese classical plays, there are certain differences. Throughout this book we are reminded that notwithstanding the degeneration of Buddhism into Lamaism, there continued to exist a deeply spiritual Buddhism, but its influence became of less and less importance with the passing of time.

LAO-TSZE O EL UNIVERSALISMO MAGICO

(Lao-Tszé or the Magical Universe)[6]

Lao-Tszé, the first essay of the book *China,* published as a separate volume in 1952, gives us something of the biography of the founder of Taoism. Few authenticated facts about his life exist. Dr. Marin, blessed with a humanistic as well as a scientific education, versed in French, Spanish, and English literatures, neglects neither the materialistic nor the occult phases of Taoism.

In a very general way Lao-Tszé's philosophy was that of non-involvement. Man is insignificant and at his best can influence nature very little. Lao-Tszé did not care to be surrounded by disciples. Fortunately for those interested in comparative religions, Lao-Tszé wrote the *Taoist Bible,* the *Tao Teh-king (Dissertation Referring to the Just Principle and Its Action),* a document which, according to Dr. Marin, is of extremely difficult interpretation. This very difficulty and therefore diversity of interpretations allowed later followers to develop Taoism in ways never dreamed of by Lao-Tszé. With the passing of time Taoist monks became very numerous, some remaining dedicated to the master's principles and others interested only in their own advantages.

It must not be assumed that followers of Lao-Tszé did not feel that man has a right, maybe a duty, to mold his surroundings. Some of the greatest plant-breeders and botanists of the world were Taoists and mankind owes them much because their science has produced plants that have helped to feed the multitudes. In spite of the value we find in Juan Marin's presentation of the Taoist doctrines, we discuss them only briefly, for we are interested in the author primarily as a creative writer.

CONFUCIO O EL HUMANISMO DIDACTIZANTE

(Confucius or Didactic Humanism)[7]

Kung Fu-tszú is better known and more historical facts about his life exist than about Lao-Tszé. Confucius' birth and death dates are given in all encyclopedias; for Lao-Tszé only the approximate date of his life (600 B.C.) is recognized.

According to Dr. Marin, the basis for the teaching of Confucius was: "All people are born good; evil is attained through man's unwillingness to submit to moral laws." The two most important factors in maintaining this pristine and fundamental goodness are: a) to have a good example set by the ruler, hence the lifelong hope of Confucius to be the close adviser to the emperor, and b) to receive an education—to learn under great teachers. Confucius actively sought contacts with the people, rulers, and movements of his time. As soon as he felt that he was ready to teach, he accepted disciples, and it is estimated that he had as many as three thousand of these. In Dr. Marin's presentation of each of the three great philosopher-teachers, Lao-Tszé, Confucius, and Buddha, we note the poetry of his prose. This does not interfere with the accuracy of his reporting nor the seriousness of his purposes. To make only one reference to our author's almost lyrical descriptions, we cite a fairly long passage almost at the end of this book, translating only a few lines into English but copying in our *General Notes* nearly all of the original Spanish. Any translation will give only a vague idea of the poetry of the description.

The Temple of Confucius in Peking

In the shadow of robust, old cypress trees which were planted by the Mongolian emperors back in the twelfth century of the Christian era, one may see today in a quiet corner of the busy Tartar city the red walls and the yellow roofs of the 'Kung Miao' or 'Temple of Kung.'[8]

After analyzing carefully the teachings of Confucius, showing how his followers modified them somewhat, and how they were influenced by Taoism and Buddhism, Dr. Marin gives us a concise statement of these teachings in a few short paragraphs—we paraphrase:

All in all the teaching of Confucius is a formidable system of ethics, sobered by ritualism and ennobled by high,

but restrained impulses of universal fraternity, not equality.
Let us not look for any mystical ecstasy nor concessions
to the Evil Spirit. It is only a body of positive doctrines,
designed to improve the state of things on earth, without
great or little concern about the Hereafter, except for a
reverence for ancestors.[9]

BUDA O LA NEGACION DEL MUNDO

(Buddha or the Rejection of the World)[10]

Buda, which made up the longest and perhaps the most important part of *China,* is a fitting climax to Dr. Marin's study
of the Big Three: Lao-Tszé, Confucius, and Buddha. After out-
lining Buddha's biography and weeding out most of the miraculous, Dr. Marin gives us a picture of the evolution of this man's
philosophy of life to a sort of religion, which gradually developed
into the cult that spread over nearly all of Asia. This dissemina-
tion was made easier because some of the preachings and examples
of Buddha were built on earlier Far-Eastern, especially Indian,
philosophies. Gradually Buddha came to the decision that peace
and spiritual happiness must be sought separately from the pomp
and circumstances of political preferment. Much is made of the
famous walks of this young prince in which he is made conscious
of the sufferings of his fellow man.

The Brahmans, leaders of the Caste System, were not friendly
to the insistence of Buddha on universal brotherhood. His message appealed to outcasts, those whose social and political status
placed them in a position below classification. But the most important contribution of Buddhism to Asia, according to Dr. Marin,
was its commandment concerning the absolute respect for life
in any form whatsoever.

A great leader, with the personality which evidently Buddha
had, is tempted by his followers to perfect an organization that
will carry down through the ages the essence of his philosophies.
Buddha, like most religious leaders of the Far East, had no concept of a second and more spiritual life. The apparent contra-

diction of Buddhism is its denial of the permanent existence of individuality and the affirmation of Karma. Reincarnation was explained by the parable of a flame in a lamp, burning through the night—a flame which while still the same appears to be different at each instance. Buddha's main teaching was that one must seek perfection and purification through meditation and that the greatest happiness is the passing of the individual soul into the oversoul, into Nirvana.

It is easy to understand why Dr. Marin, whose concern in all fields of art, including music, was second only to his interest in *belles lettres* and philosophy, should make reference to the development of statuary and architecture insofar as Buddhism encouraged it.

At the end of this very interesting book in a short chapter with the title "Final," our author sums up in some of his poetic prose the essence of Buddhism. We recommend to those who read Spanish the whole of this section. We quote in our *General Notes* several paragraphs of Juan Marin's beautiful composition. A few lines are paraphrased here:

> Taken in its essence and with all the variations that it has suffered in the last twenty-five centuries, the message of Buddha is a moral one filled with intense poetical and emotional elements. . . .
>
> Buddhism created ethico-esthetic complexities of un- equalled beauty. The serenity of the youthful countenance of the god, the supreme harmony of his body in repose are equations of the purest theoanthropomorphic beauty.[11]

Dr. Marin makes specific reference to the rapid assimilation and acceptance of Buddhism in China:

> Buddhism in China was not a religion of the educated nor of the mandarins as was Confucianism, nor did it take a direction toward the laboratory of the astrologer-alchemist as did Taoism. It was, from the moment it entered into contact with the Chinese people, a religion of the humble and a consolation for the hopeless.[12]

In our desire to present Juan Marin as a creative writer and thinker, we have tried to show that he was sympathetic to all attempts to reach the ultimate truth. We say "attempts to reach the ultimate truth," for few will claim that it can be reached. Dr. Marin quotes several times in this book and repeats on the last page an Oriental proverb: "Many roads lead to the summit of the mountain, but the moon which is seen from the top is always the same."

Dr. Marin goes on to say, "The roads are the various schools, sects, and religious orders that flourish in the Far East, seeking the final truth, that which Max Muller describes vaguely as the notion of the "infinite" and which the Japanese G. Kotto defines as "The consciousness of having contact with God."

Again, to end his book, Dr. Marin repeats the proverb: "But the moon which is seen from the top is always the same."

EL ALMA DE CHINA

(The Soul of China)[13]

El alma . . . is one of the longest as well as the most scholarly of Dr. Marin's books under the general classification of *Civilization*. The reader who has enjoyed Havelock Ellis' masterly publication, *The Soul of Spain*, will not be surprised to observe a similarity in the contents of these two interpretations of interesting peoples.

Fortunately, there was available to Marin one of the world's greatest collections of books on China and other countries of the Far East, mostly in French and English, languages he knew well. Since the Marins were virtually prisoners of the Japanese for several months, Dr. Marin used that time of enforced inactivity to work on his publications. He makes reference to this in his book, *La India eterna:*

> We cannot fail to recall those moments, now so long
> past, when surrounded by Japanese soldiers on all sides,
> we were working in China intensely and passionately, so
> as to forget the blood and horror that were all around us,

> on our study of Chinese Buddhism that was to have a place
> afterwards in our book *China*.[14]

It is said that a lofty mountain is always a challenge to the
alpinist; so a new country, especially such an enigmatic and
poorly understood one as China, was a challenge to Dr. Marin
who spent many hours of tireless research during one of the most
interesting and trying times possible.

Here the treatment of *El alma de China* must be brief. It is
hoped, nevertheless, that our suggestions will inspire readers to
study the whole for themselves. We group together those chapters dealing with Chinese literature but make references to others.

These are:

Poesía (Poetry) . . .	Chapter I. p. 17 ff.
Teatro (Drama) . . .	Chapter VI. p. 239 ff.
"El sueño de la cámara roja," joya de la novelística china . . .	Chapter X. p. 365 ff.
(The Red Chamber Dream, the jewel of Chinese literature)	
La novela china contemporánea, *Pa Kin* y *Mao Toen*, sus dos más altos exponentes . .	Chapter XI. p. 377 ff.
(Chinese contemporary novel, *Pa Kin* and *Mao Toen*, her two highest exponents)	

Under *Poetry* Dr. Marin makes reference to poetic drama, but
in spite of his faithful presentation of this, we are impressed
more deeply by the beautiful short poems that have a certain
resemblance to the Japanese *Haikai*. He mentions the fact that
the emotional element in Chinese literature is usually more subdued than in Occidental productions.

We paraphrase a few lines from Dr. Marin's beautiful translation of a short poem by Li-Po, the best known of the Chinese
poets:

NOSTALGIA

> Seen from my couch
> The moon spreads out
> Its crystal frost upon the land.

I lift my eyes to see the shining star;
I think about my native town
And then, I bow my head . . .[15]

For the more scientifically minded, there are a few pages that discuss the Chinese language, in which we are informed of the importance of tonality in its poetry.

Even for persons who have visited the Chinese theatre in New York City or in San Francisco, our author's discussion of dramatic literature is very revealing. Like those who have been brought up on the Occidental theatrical tradition, Dr. Marin finds much that happens during a representation of a classical Chinese drama a bit perplexing. But as with other matters that are very different from that to which he was accustomed, he tries to appreciate the theatre from the Chinese point of view. In *El alma de China* as well as in *Mesa de mah-jong* he gives a resumé of a classical play, "La cámara del oeste" (The Western Room), with generous selections translated into Spanish. A few things that he cannot accept in the classical Chinese theatre are: a) the use of men for women's roles, b) the orchestra that adds nothing to the performance and, c) the confusion that exists in the theatre while the actors present the play.

Of Chinese literature, according to Dr. Marin, the novel is the least artistic. One classical and two contemporary novels are discussed. He attributes the near-failure of the novel to two main causes. First, Confucius taught that man ought to keep the emotions under control; and secondly, the novel needs an everyday, down-to-earth language instead of the extremely artificial literary Chinese used in artistic writing. He also provides us with a translation of a few scenes from "Historia de la guitarra" (History of the Guitar).

Parenthetically, we should like to suggest that if one were to collect all of Dr. Marin's translations from English and French sources to Spanish poetry, he would be able to assemble a book equal in length to *Looping,* much of it really inspired.

In the chapter "Pintura" our author mentions the interdependence of calligraphy and painting. To make the ideographs so exactly and artistically, as they are often seen displayed on scrolls, requires the same patience and careful workmanship as the illuminations of our medieval manuscripts. The chapter "Jade," semi-imaginative, has served as the basis for one of Dr. Marin's monographs in English which he read as a lecture in Cairo, Egypt in 1948.[16]

We have remarked previously that Juan Marin had a great passion for music. The chapter on Chinese music and his explanation of the origin and evolution of the five-toned scale are important as is the discussion of the various instruments used in China. His report of attending a concert by a native Chinese orchestra is instructive and revealing. The remarks on the trend in China to use Occidental style of music and instruments deserve special attention. Invitations that the Marins received to attend cultural affairs, invitations not normally extended to foreigners, prove that they made a place for themselves wherever they happened to be stationed.

There is much to explain the culture and customs of China in the chapters on Architecture, The Dragon Myth, and Footbinding. In the chapter "China y occidente" (China and the Western World), we are informed with documentation that China has been isolated from the West only at intervals. The Greeks, the Romans, and the Arabs carried on commerce with China long before the famous expedition of Marco Polo in the thirteenth century.

The chapter "Las ruinas de Angkor" (The Ruins of Angkor), also mentioned in *Mesa de mah-jong,* is one of our author's best descriptions of a visit to an historical site. Leaving aside the well-documented account of the discovery of these ruins, we find especially lyrical the paragraph with which Dr. Marin ends this book:

> Two or three times a year, during the great religious festivals, the royal dancing girls of Phnom-Penh come to the ruins to fulfill certain religious rites and then, on that

magnificent terrace which extends in front of the west
door of the Angkor-Vat Palace, they dance in groups, to
the rhythm of stringed instruments.[17]

Thus *El alma de China* remains Dr. Marin's major work designed to give us a complete picture of *The Land of the Dragon*.

MESA DE MAH-JONG

(Mah-Jong Table)

Of the books on China, *La mesa de mah-jong*[18] comes the nearest
to being creative writing, making more use of the imagination,
hence being more poetical, although even in the most scientific
of his writings, Dr. Marin could not be entirely prosaic. He ob-
serves realistically, but writes imaginatively, especially in *Mesa
de mah-jong*. Perhaps the "Prologue" gives the proper tone to the
whole book:

Walking through the streets of a city in China means
challenging an avalanche of varied sensorial impressions.
Of course it is necessary to confront all the odors, all the
sights, all the sounds imaginable. In China the street is
comprehensive; people live and die on it and there are
also cases when life begins in the middle of the street. . . .
Among the thousand and one sounds, there is something
like *ta-ta-ta-ta-* of a machine gun coming through an open
window or a door left partly ajar. One hears this *ta-ta* more
frequently in those sections where there are many tea-
rooms and restaurants but it may be heard nearly any
place. It is the rattle of a hard object striking against a
wooden surface. . . . It has to do with a pastime, one of
the most innocent, the famous mah-jong of the Chinese. . . .
Mesa de mah-jong is therefore the title of this book. There
is in it variety, color, and noise. Let us play a record of
impressions with the good-natured reader. If he does not
become bored with the first deal of the pieces, we can
play and play, more and more, up to the end of the book,
that is to say, until dawn surprises us . . . just like the
Chinese players in a noisy tea-house of Shanghai or
Peking.[19]

Mesa de mah-jong is divided into a *Prólogo* and seven main divisions as follows:

Primera Parte (First Part)	:	Arte y literatura de China (Art and Literature of China)
Parte Segunda (Second Part)	:	Filosofía, religiones, festivales y costumbres (Philosophy, Religions, Festivals, and Customs)
Parte Tercera (Third Part)	:	Mitos y leyendas (Myths and Legends)
Parte Cuarta (Fourth Part)	:	Sitios y monumentos (Places and Monuments)
Parte Quinta (Fifth Part)	:	De la medicina (Concerning Medicine)
Parte Sexta (Sixth Part)	:	De la historia (Concerning History)
Parte Séptima (Seventh Part)	:	Crónica de oriente (Chronicles of the Orient)

Part I is of extraordinary interest because Dr. Marin was essentially a man of letters. Of the Chinese novel *Chin ping mei* (in Spanish *Oro, vaso, ciruelas* and in English *The Golden Vase of Plums*), our author says, ". . . they assure us that the best way to know and understand the soul of China is to read *The Golden Vase of Plums*." The English translation has been widely read, according to Dr. Marin.[20] He reports that one of the most popular of the Chinese plays, *La cámara del oeste (The Western Room)*, has also been quite popular in English having had a run of more than three hundred performances in England alone.

In the chapter on "The Status of Woman in China," Dr. Marin translates to Spanish a poem that is the lament of one of the fair sex. We paraphrase a few lines and include a longer selection in Spanish in our *General Notes:*

> Oh! How sad it is to be a woman!
> Nothing on earth is less esteemed
>
> . . . . . .
>
> When a daughter is born no one is happy
> The parents take no notice of her birth
> She grows up in the darkness of the inner rooms.[21]

In Part II, Dr. Marin relates that at the beginning of the 19th century a movement called "Renaissance" attempted to eradicate Confucianism and that China came very near to being converted to Nestorian Christianity, in what is known as the Taiping Revolt, in 1851.

After discussing myths and legends of China, the most amusing and interesting being "El origin de los zancudos" (The Origin of the Mosquitoes), our author describes in "Lugares y monumentos" (Places and Monuments) journeys made into Indo-China. We find exceptionally provocative and charming what is recorded under "El embrujo de Peking" (The Charm of Peking).

In the short section "De la historia" (Concerning History), the most enlightening essays are "Los pies vendados" (Foot Binding) and the nefarious influences of the eunuchs. Dr. Marin, as a man of science and with advanced medical training, could not fail to make many references to alchemy and medicine.

The last section is a miscellany treating a number of non-related subjects, the most interesting of which we recommend to those fortunate enough to be well acquainted with Spanish. "La respuesta de Dios" (God's Answer) shows again that when religious beliefs are concerned, Dr. Marin maintains his sympathy and open-mindedness. "Perder cara" (To lose face) explains very graphically the lengths to which Chinese and other Orientals will go to save face. He reports personal experiences which make his explanation even more vivid.

In a short study like this we have had to pass over many fine bits of writing. If one were to try to separate those parts that may easily be considered creative writing, including short stories, legends, and poems, an interesting and artistic collection could be made. Especially are we attracted to "La doncella de la gran campana" (The Maiden of the Great Bell), "El Buda de jade" (The Jade Buddha)—which although only a description is a real prose poem, and the humorous "Una visión canaánica" (A Canaanic Vision). This does not mean that other selections will not have greater appeal to some readers.

In conclusion we should like to say, "He who wishes to know China by way of reading a relatively short and imaginatively written book may well begin with *Mesa de mah-jong*. If he desires to have a more complete and detailed knowledge, without passing years in that enigmatic and awakening country, let him read *El alma de China*."

It is easily seen that Juan Marin was profoundly interested in all that concerned China. Although he has shown in his writings a determination to know about other countries, Egypt, India, El Salvador and the United States, his attitude toward China seems somehow to show greater depth. He had without doubt hoped to spend years at his diplomatic post in Shanghai; he began soon after his arrival in the *Land of the Dragon* to investigate every aspect of that intriguing, mysterious, and baffling land: its geography, its history, and its literature and above all its religions and philosophies. His first book concerning Old Cathay was given the title of *China* (1944) but its sub-title, *Lao-Tszé, Confucio, y Buda* is much more indicative of its contents for it is a conscientious study of these three religious leaders and philosophers. *El alma de China* (1945) and *Mesa de mah-jong* (1948) soon followed *China* and contain a wider variety of subject matter, for *China* was written from a library before Dr. Marin had been able to see things for himself. With the beginning of the retreat of the Japanese armies the Marins were able to travel more extensively. It is quite possible that these three books were being prepared simultaneously but to finish the two later books, books of more general interest, more than library research was needed. While finishing his studies of Lao-Tszé, Confucius, and Buddha, besides reading hundreds of books in a local library, mainly books in French and English, Dr. Marin had frequent conversations with a Buddhist sage who helped the young diplomat understand the *Big Three*.

The purely intellectual research needed for the termination of *China* had to be supplemented by travel for the more personal points of view found in his next two books, *El alma* . . . and

Mesa . . . , but months of reading were essential for these two also.

Fortunately or unfortunately in this chapter we find no comments on Chinese communism; the Marins were asked to assume diplomatic duties in Egypt and India before the present regime came to power. We know from his other writings that Dr. Marin was a strong believer in democracy and liberty and are therefore able to guess what his reactions would have been to some of the extremes of communism in China. But leaving international politics aside, we cannot refrain from expressing our gratitude to the author of such revealing, penetrating publications as *El alma de China* and *Mesa de mah-jong*. Now that a more cosmopolitan attitude is making itself felt, it is our hope that translations to English and French, at least, will be prepared.

CHAPTER V

Travel and Interpretation

Two of Juan Marin's books: *El Egipto de los faraones (Egypt of the Pharaohs)* and *La India eterna (Eternal India)* are separated for discussion from the group considered under the heading "Philosophies, Religions, and Civilization" because *El Egipto . . .* and *La India . . .* emphasize travel primarily even though much space is given in them to religions and philosophies. There is also some travel and interpretation in works studied in Chapter IV.

When Dr. Marin entered the diplomatic services he did not cease his literary activities. To his never-ceasing desire to write he added a determination to document himself thoroughly for the demanding duties as a diplomatic representative of his country and it is agreed that his contributions as a diplomat were outstanding. He became more than superficially acquainted with all the countries to which he was assigned: China, El Salvador, Egypt, and India. His compulsion to write resulted in many books and articles about these lands.

Not all of the members of a diplomatic corps care to learn and to write so conscientiously about the countries in which they are stationed; nevertheless some of Chile's representatives, often chosen from among the republic's leading writers, have continued their literary careers. A striking example is the great Chilean novelist, Alberto Blest Gana.

One often speculates, "Had Chile, as well as other nations, maintained in Egypt men with Dr. Marin's energy and abilities to discover its soul and interpret it to the world, would not the peace of the Middle East have been more secure?" When such enthusiastic, enlightened, and well-prepared representatives can be found, everything possible ought to be done to keep them at their posts.

It goes without saying that Dr. Marin had a great sympathy and love for China. He would gladly have remained in that very challenging country, but when offered an assignment in Egypt he willingly accepted. Egypt and her ancient civilizations had always been close to the heart of the author of *Paralelo 53 sur*.

EL EGIPTO DE LOS FARAONES[1]

(Egypt of the Pharaohs)

El Egipto . . . presents the romantic Land of the Nile in a semi-popular manner. This publication has maintained a surprising popularity, having merited several editions, the third published in 1963 being the one we have used. It has some of the qualities already pointed out in *El alma de China* but in a few respects it represents a slightly changed although not a radical departure, depending to a greater extent on travel. There are pages that emphasize the lyrical and creative abilities of the writer without detracting from the authenticity of the whole. In his "Introduction" Dr. Marin indicates the scope of his treatment of Egypt:

> This is, then, a book that attempts to deal principally with the Egypt of the Pharaohs. Incidentally there enter into it some modern and collateral themes. This does not change, however, the fundamental purpose of the work, which is that of presenting a synthesis of the impressions and visions gathered together by us during our years of residence in the *Land of the Nile,* of the four great plateaux or layers of culture that superimposed themselves one above the other during the course of Egyptian history: the Pharaonic, the Greek or Greco-roman, the Coptic, and the Islamic. We have interested ourselves essentially in the first three with no wish to minimize the last that has given and continues to give great artistic treasures and powerful reserves of faith and courage.[2]

Dr. Marin acknowledges his debt to the egyptologists whose works he uses extensively but excuses himself for not appending a bibliography. We have noted that *El Egipto de los faraones,* although sympathetically written, is authoritative and well documented, but our interest will be concentrated on the creative aspects that constantly appeal to the non-scientific reader. For example, references to "Sindbad, the Sailor," "Helen of Troy," and to the snake charmer are worthy of our author's best creative efforts.

The use of the first person plural, frequent reference to Milena Luksic de Marín, and the inclusion of both the Marins in some of the illustrations add a certain intimacy to the factual material that of itself is never lacking in interest. Some of the places visited give the author greater opportunities than others to write semi-poetically. The confrontation with the Sphinx early in the book, the presentation of the temples at Luxor, the description of the trip to the Siwa Oasis with its references to a similar excursion of Alexander the Great, and finally the visit to the Monastery of Saint Catherine bring forth creative writing as well as realistic reporting.

It is quite natural that Juan Marín, a recognized poet, should dedicate many pages to *belles lettres*. To illustrate this we reproduce in an excellent English translation a few lines from an early Egyptian poet. In our *General Notes* we transcribe several lines in Dr. Marín's translation of this same poem to Spanish:

> Death faces me today
> as convalescence after sickness
> as a garden entered after rising
>
> . . . . .
>
> Death faces me today
> as the perfume of open lotus flowers
> as water calms a man's thirst
>
> . . . . .
>
> Death faces me today
> as the landscape of his native town
> to the man who has been a prisoner
> and returns at last to his own land[3]
>
> . . . . .

To give some relief from these thoughts on death, Dr. Marín

discusses the place of love and the high esteem in which women were held in Egypt.

There is a theme that runs through several of Dr. Marin's books on the Middle and Far East, that dramatic literature did not have its earliest examples in Greece, but that Chinese and Egyptian national drama were centuries old before the time of Aristotle. We find his arguments quite convincing. As in the early dramatic literature of Europe, Egypt's plays were both religious and secular, but the religious element was always present. Additional references to drama are a citation in Spanish prose from a play that begins, "I am Isis. . . ."[4] and again another, a beautiful poetic translation from "Retorno de Seth" (The Return of Seth) in which he uses a non-metered, non-rhyming verse form.[5]

In the chapter "Escultura faraónica" (Pharaohnic Sculpture) Dr. Marin explains that the Egyptians had no taboo against the representation of the human body, hence the early development of sculpture whereas only relatively late in India was the human body considered a legitimate subject for statuary.

In his chapter "Vida, pasión y muerte de Cleopatra" (Life, Suffering and Death of Cleopatra), Dr. Marin makes the last three centuries before Christ live for us as he rehabilitates the much maligned empress. This chapter offers exceptional opportunities for semi-imaginative writing, opportunities not neglected by Juan Marin who while making use of his imagination continued to write with veracity and documentation.

Passing over his discussion of "Puerto Said" (Port Said) which gives Dr. Marin occasion to tell the history of the canal and to present what he considers to be the legitimate Egyptian claims for the management of this waterway, we find much of interest in the final pages, "Siguiendo las huellas de Moisés" (Following the Footsteps of Moses). Again, as he gives a resumé of the Biblical history of the great Jewish leader, our author shows his openmindedness as he makes a very human individual of the man who saved the Hebrew Children from their Egyptian Captivity.

Of the "Epilogue" the last paragraph is worth quoting:

> And now, benevolent reader, we must separate. There is perhaps only one lesson worth learning, among many others of passing significance, one that we ought to learn from this book: and it is that mankind, from the beginning of its history, being mortal has always wanted to live as immortal.[6]

Unfortunately, *El Egipto* . . . , like many excellent books written in Spanish, is not as well known in English speaking countries as it deserves. No work that we have read concerning the *Land of the Pharaohs* has given us such a clear insight both into the ancient and the modern civilizations of Egypt.

LA INDIA ETERNA[7]

(Eternal India)

La India eterna is Dr. Marin's longest book, of slightly less than five hundred closely printed pages, profusely illustrated with photographs usually prepared by Milena Luksic de Marin who also provided most of the illustrative material for *El Egipto de los faraones.*

In the author's "Introduction" we are told that the Marins spent four years in India, in addition to an earlier visit in 1947 on the occasion of the celebration of the independence of that country from England. It is possible that a few lines from this *Introducción* translated to English and a longer quotation in Spanish will set the stage for the whole book:

> In four years of sojourn in the Land of the Ganges we traveled over its extensive territories from the slopes of the Himalayas to the Cape of Comorin, from Assam to Kashmir, from Darjeeling to Trivandrum, from Madras to Udaipur.[8]

The Marins had arrived in India for their first visit coming from China and the Philippines but this, their second visit, coming from Egypt by way of the Suez Canal, the Red Sea, the Gulf of Aden, and the Arabian Sea, was a new and unforgettable experience. After a brief discussion of Bombay, our author hurries on from this modern commercial center to the more poetic treatment of Agra with its world famous Taj-Mahal, which he says is above comparison with any other architectural marvel of the world, although Dr. Marin cannot forget the beauties of the Temple of Heaven in Peking nor the ruins of Angkor-Vat of Cambodia. From the chapter "El Taj-Mahal" we paraphrase a few lines and recommend the whole as one of the great presentations of this architectural wonder of the world:

> Because the Taj is the poem of love built by the Emperor Shaw Jehan in memory of his wife, Muntaz Mahal, or in other words "The Lady of the Taj."[9]

From the point of view of the development of Buddhism, the chapter "Asoka el Grande" is very important. Dr. Marin has insisted in his earlier book, *Buda o la negación del mundo*, on the significance of Asoka in the history of Buddhism. While visiting the Buddhist temple, "La Stupa de Sanchi," the author again remarks on the importance of Asoka in the rapid spread of Buddhism during the third and second centuries before Christ.

The description of the visit to Benares, the most sacred spot in India, where multitudes come to bathe in the Ganges and many to die there, to be cremated, and to have their ashes thrown into the sacred waters, reminds us of a famous description of the same place by Vicente Blasco Ibáñez.[10] But Blasco saw only the fanaticism and the filth, whereas Dr. Marin always sympathized with religious beliefs even when the scene might be unlovely. Both men, however, are masters of the art of vivid description.

Throughout *La India . . .* we marvel at the illustrations provided by Milena Luksic de Marin for this book as well as for *El Egipto de los faraones.* Even when printed on ordinary paper they add greatly to the understanding of the text, and the inclusion at times of photographs of Dr. Marin or Milena herself often helps to give one a better idea of the proportions of buildings, statues, etc. A detailed report on all the chapters of this book is obviously impossible. For that reason we refer our readers to the original publication, *La India eterna,* which seems to be written with exceptional understanding and sympathy; it is one of Dr. Marin's most appealing and imaginative works.

Although Dr. Marin has reported accurately on the architectural wonders of India, his discussions of the great mystics and philosophers are even more interesting. Outstanding is the account of a visit of the Marins with Maharichi Ramana, accompanied by their great friend Adelina del Carril, widow of the famous author of *Don Segundo Sombra,* Ricardo Güiraldes. Those who will accept no truths reached through extrasensory perception may scoff at some of this report that seems to accept intuition, telepathy, etc., as legitimate evidence of communication. There is a chapter on Sri Aurobindo, called "The Saint of Pondicherry." Dr. Marin mentions the fact that Gabriela Mistral (Chile's winner of the Nobel Prize for Literature in 1945) and Pearl Buck nominated Aurobindo for the 1950 Nobel Prize which, however, was awarded that year to the American poet living in England, T. S. Eliot. Aurobindo's philosophy was that man must continue his upward climb toward perfection in spite of any temporary setback. Such a philosophy appealed to Dr. Marin who was an optimist that realized that there is hope for humanity, however unlovely and degraded man may seem. These two chapters, together with those on Gandhi and Tagore, are exceedingly significant, for they represent, as Dr. Marin states: action, word, knowledge, and intuition.

The chapter "Un himno a Siva" (A Hymn to Siva) gives another of Dr. Marin's renditions of a poem, this one dating from 1400 B.C. Of this composition we paraphrase a quatrain and transcribe a longer section in our *General Notes:*

> Wearing in his hair embellished with fragrant flowers,
> the golden disc of the moon
> this god dances in the beautiful Vadougour
> and bestows on me his grace and his love.[11]

Of great interest is the report on temples seen during the pilgrimage of the Marins to the southern tip of India, Cape Comorin, and to the islands of Rameswaran and Ceylon. The myth or tradition of the Monkey-god is mentioned in this section of the book in connection with the spreading of Buddhism to Ceylon. In the chapter "La isla sagrada de Rameswaran" Dr. Marin treats us with another of his exceptionally beautiful descriptions.[12]

Readers find refreshing the jump from Ceylon, in the very hot climate of the far south, to Darjeeling, the summer resort in the foothills of the Himalayas. There is a long chapter dealing with Kashmir, a city that seems to have had a special place in the affections of the Marins. Is this because it has some of the same beauties as those so justly praised in their beloved Chile? At any rate the lakes, the mountains, and the hospitality of the people are constantly extolled. Even the religio-philosophical environment seems here more provocative to Dr. Marin. He makes much of his meeting with Dr. Chaterjee who held the thesis that Christ had been on earth before the historical date of His birth and had been in Kashmir and that His real burial place is in Srinagar. Here as in several other parts of *La India eterna* Dr. Marin uses the term *monismo,* seemingly interested in the idea that all people everywhere are seeking God and although the roads followed may differ, eventually all converge on the same ultimate truth.

There are in *La India* . . . several religio-philosophical interpolations, but our author ends with what he calls "Una historia mitad real, mitad imaginativa" (A Half True, Half Imaginative Story). It is the famous rope-trick in which a fakir causes a rope to shoot up into the air and a boy to climb it into the clouds. This fictional aside might well have been included in any one of his collections of short stories.

In both of these books discussed under the heading of "Travel and Interpretation" we are conscious of the dual personality of Dr. Marin: the careful student-reporter and the creative writer. At times one shows through more than the other, but on the whole he has maintained a careful and artistic balance between them.

Of the two publications more discussion has been devoted to *La India* for several reasons. In the first place *La India . . .* is at least one third longer than *El Egipto. . . .* In the second place, in spite of Dr. Marin's evident interest in history, even pre-history, his lifelong concern has been mankind. In a country of thinkers and philosophers, like India, dozens of religious leaders and mystics are always willing to meet and converse with inquiring and intellectual seekers-after-truth.

It is quite evident that Dr. Marin made little distinction between religion and philosophy. Toward the end of *La India eterna* the following succinct statement sums up this religio-philosophical stance:

> And when we say schools of philosophy we mean to include also religion, for in India religion is not theology but philosophy.[13]

On reading the publications discussed in Chapter V we became increasingly aware of the effort, inspiration, and sympathy with which they were assembled. Both *El Egipto . . .* and *La India . . .* are important additions to the literature concerning these two countries but we feel that *La India . . .* , besides its value as an aid to the understanding of the Land of Ghandi, reveals more of the characteristics of the author than does *El Egipto. . . .* This latter publication has had more editions than the former and, we are told, is often used as a text or important reference book for elementary schools, but we find *La India . . .* more appealing. Why? Possibly because the author, being deeply interested in literature, art, philosophies, and religions, found many kindred spirits in every place that he visited. Hundreds of leaders in these fields were always willing, even eager, to discuss the relevance of these subjects to modern problems.

Dr. Marin was an ideal traveler and observer, for in spite of annoyances and inconveniences, and these always confront the voyager whether he be in the New World or the Old World, in the highly developed or in the under-privileged countries, he accepted existing conditions with patience and equanimity. As a successful diplomat he seemed to accept quietly what he met and only to ask himself, "Why do such things exist?" One Mexican diplomat, probably not too well liked, traveled accompanied by his own cook who prepared each morning the *tortillas* that are part of every breakfast in Mexico. This Dr. Marin would never do. This attitude of acceptance of things as they are made him a welcomed visitor and gained for him and his country innumerable friends.

CHAPTER VI

Medical Writings

It is not surprising that Dr. Marin published articles, books, and essays dealing with medicine in its various phases. Although later he made the difficult decisions, first to enter the medical branch of the navy and later to offer his services to his country in the diplomatic corps, he never lost his interest in his first love, medicine; it meant only that he was temporarily ceasing active private practice. During his several assignments in the Chilean diplomatic corps he was in close contact with local doctors' organizations and societies of interest to persons engaged in health activities. In this section of our review we comment briefly on several of Dr. Marin's medical writings published in four books, passing over his dissertation with only a short note.[1]

Dr. Marin's first serious writing in the field of medicine was his doctoral dissertation, *La tiro-toxicosis y su tratamiento quirúgico*.[2] This was written specifically to satisfy the requirement in Chile, at the time, that all candidates for the medical degree prepare a study. It makes no pretense of literary style. We do glimpse, however, evidences of good writing that later became his trademark.

CLINICAS Y MAESTROS EN INGLATERRA Y FRANCIA

(Clinics and Professors in England and France)

Skipping over *La tiro-toxicosis* . . . we shall discuss first *Clínicas* . . . which, to quote from the *Prólogo,* is ". . . some travel notes jotted down a few months ago, hurriedly and superficially, during a trip through Europe."[3] In the same prologue Juan Marin says further, "It is my intention to offer sketches of men and institutions written while in the very surroundings in which they carry on their work."[4]

He began his tour of medical schools at the University of Dublin with the intention to move from Ireland to Scotland, to visit Edinburgh and Glasgow, thence to continue to London, and finally to end his sojourn in Paris with side trips to Geneva and Germany.

Although this publication has a serious and primarily scientific purpose—to learn everything possible about hospitals and professors of medicine—the young physician-poet could not resist the temptation to report on the beauties of the places he visited; some of these reports become quite lyrical. Of this tendency we cite a few lines, paraphrased in English and include a longer quotation in Spanish in our *General Notes:*

> For me Edinburgh is one of the most beautiful cities
> in the world. It has the misty and barbarous beauty of a
> Rome built on the edge of the northern limits of Europe.[5]

Besides giving us a condensed history of the beginnings and the evolution of medical schools, Dr. Marin writes about some of the great men of medicine, e.g., Robert Liston, James Syme, Joseph Lister, and others. He was obviously quite interested in the first use of anesthetics and in antiseptic surgery. A quite modern operating room attracted the attention of our young M.D. Procedures there carried over to descriptions of operations in his novels—a notable one being in *Margarita, el aviador y el médico.*

Meeting the great leaders whose lives he had studied in the Medical School of the University of Chile was a never-to-be-forgotten experience for the young surgeon. He reports on several of these, one of the most complete being a long interview with Dr. Pauchet.[6] In the section "Sketches de la facultad de Paris," Dr. Marin mentions nineteen famous professors, mainly surgeons.

It has already been noted more than once that Juan Marin, in spite of being a true man of science, accepted the premise that there are things that science cannot and ought not try to analyze. In a most revealing chapter of *Clínicas . . . ,* he reports on a book by Professor Dr. Binet-Danglé, *La Folie de Jésus (The Insanity of Jesus).*[7] He agrees with a chaplain, with whom he discussed the book, who stated: "Let us not destroy the only consoling light that is left to our souls."[8]

One chapter speaks of the history and importance of the *Museo militar del hospital de Val-de-Grace (Military Museum of the Val-de-Grace Hospital).* The most practical chapters are those dealing respectively with the effects of speed, physical and mental conditions, and other factors concerning the selection and training of military aviators.

Clínicas . . . ends with a description of a visit to a leper colony and with remarks by Dr. Marin on ways to improve the leprosarium maintained by Chile on the Easter Islands.

POLIEDRO MEDICO[9]

(Medical Miscellany)

The first chapters of this book are the introductory lectures given during the time that Juan Marin held the position of Professor of the History of Medicine in the Medical School of the University of Chile in Santiago. The other chapters are articles, essays on outstanding contributors to medical science, and speeches given on various occasions mainly on medical subjects. Only one item, a greeting to the famous Spanish novelist, critic, and essayist, Ramón Gómez de la Serna, who was honored by a luncheon at a meeting of the Society of Surgeons on November 27, 1931, is definitely non-medical.

The author calls the essays in *Poliedro médico,* "Diversas y heterogéneas facetas" (Diverse and Heterogeneous Facets). Although only thirty-three years of age at the time of the publishing of *Poliedro* . . . , Dr. Marin had had many varied experiences. He says, "Our curiosity had caused us to draw near the most varied fountains of learning and sensibility."[10]

The opening lecture by a new professor and particularly if the course also is a new one is a very important event. In our opinion the first chapter in *Poliedro* . . . could well serve as a model for such a gala occasion. We give the complete title although it is quite long:

> *Introducción al estudio de la Historia de la Medicina. Lección inaugural dictada en la Universidad de Chile el 25 de Abril de 1932* (Introduction to the Study of the History of Medicine. Inaugural Lecture Given in the University of Chile, April 25, 1932).

We quote a few significant sentences from this lecture:

> I shall be inspired, therefore, by his (Dr. Lucas Sierra's) example and follow the traditions set by him.
>
> . . . . .
>
> I wish to thank [here Dr. Marin mentions several important people present] for the part they had in establishing this class . . . and above all I ought to thank them for the kindness with which they judged my merits and abilities when they were considering me for the professorship.
>
> I shall try to be worthy of this confidence that they have placed in me.[11]

In one of his first classroom lectures, the new professor of the History of Medicine insists on the importance of this subject ending with the statement:

> Thus the History of Medicine represents the highest teaching of medical ethics and is one of the most powerful factors in scientific progress.[12]

The chapter reporting the visit of the famous Italian professor of the History of Medicine, Arturo Castiglione, allows Dr. Marin another opportunity to express his opinion that the study of the History of Medicine has been neglected in Chile and that it is one of the most important fields. Another very interesting and important chapter of *Poliedro* . . . is "Hipócrates y el hipocratismo" (Hippocrates and Hippocratism) which covers the same material that we find in the monograph, *El origin de la medicina hipocrática (The Origin of Hippocratic Medicine)*. There are several chapters referring to famous doctors of Chile, including two in praise of Dr. Marin's favorite professor, the outstanding surgeon, Dr. Lucas Sierra.

Some of the lectures are very practical, as for example the one discussing professional secrecy in medicine and another dealing with the selection of aviation personnel. A fairly detailed account is given of the methods used in Europe to select the young men who are to be trained as military pilots. It is well to recapitulate in order to call the attention of the reader to certain beliefs held by Juan Marin having to do with the preparation of physicians. He insists that, in addition to courses already being given, the History of Medicine deserves a place in any program to prepare doctors; that a truly great doctor ought to have a solid cultural background; that a medical program should include a study of the emotions and their importance to the practicing physician.

EL PROBLEMA SEXUAL Y SUS NUEVAS FORMULAS SOCIALES[13]

(The Problem of Sex and Its New Sociological Formulas)

In the well-planned *Introducción* that Dr. Marin prepared for *El problema* . . . we read that the material included herein had appeared in previous publications. It is our understanding, also, that these earlier essays contained little that is not in *El problema*. . . . We therefore eliminate a separate discussion of his former book, *La nueva moral—Educación sexual y matrimonio controlado (The New Moral—Sex Education and Controlled Matrimony)*.[14]

Dr. Marin hesitated when faced by the task of preparing a more complete study[15] for the general public, a duty that he finally decided could not be shirked. The frank discussion of subjects almost universally taboo would, he was convinced, bring him severe and impassioned criticism. But his compassion for those who were suffering because of ignorance, especially those in his own country, Chile, encouraged him to face such unjustifiable and normal, conservative reactions. Sustained also by the advice given to students at Dartmouth college by Emerson, he says, "Por eso, sin temores escribimos estas páginas" (Therefore, without fear we write these pages). Although he wrote "without fear," he realized that much short-sighted criticism would be leveled against him. In this present book he shows an almost evangelical zeal and great moral courage in discussing the principles that he enounces.

Dr. Marin disclaims any originality for this book, but the enormous work of assembling opinions from other great thinkers and writers in this field deserves serious consideration. At least we are convinced that he had read quite widely the works of recognized authorities on the problems herein discussed so knowledgeably. The young doctor mentions such persons as Gregorio Marañón, Havelock Ellis, Bertrand Russel, Alfred Adler, Francisco de Figueroa, and Oswald Spengler, as well as lesser known Chilean experts. These appear on nearly every page. It is well to remember, however, that in spite of much international acclaim, this study was prepared primarily for Dr. Marin's own countrymen.

A basic tenet repeated and carefully developed throughout *El problema* . . . is:

> The sublimation of the physical act of love toward its intellectual meaning, the mythical symbology created around the physiological phenomenon, constitute the most beautiful stairs ever established by man. . . .[16]

Again and again throughout his writings, even the most scientific, Dr. Marin insists on another important tenet of the whole of his philosophy. Pure materialism can never be trusted; man may be basically an animal, with some of the actions of the lower ones; nevertheless he has the intelligence to spiritualize and to intellectualize even what may be considered the lower expressions of love. We quote:

> In the field of biology we are not pure materialists nor quintaessential idealists. We believe that one can no longer draw a line between the physical and the psychic.[17]

Near the end of the chapter "Enunciado," Dr. Marin announces the two goals that he pursues throughout his study: "Educación sexual," and "Matrimonio controlado."[18] The chapter "Prejucio y moral" presents an interesting history and evolution of moral codes insofar as they relate to the relative status of woman. In essence he explains that as woman becomes more independent and self-sufficient economically, she attains greater equality with man in all respects.

"La nueva moral" is a chapter that insists on a new concept of the equality of woman. Although Juan Marin's political and economic beliefs were opposed to those generally held in Russia, he recognized that that country had made great advances in the emancipation of woman. Some of these advances are listed:

> Equal responsibility of both parents for offspring.
> Establishing that no child is to be called illegitimate.
> Rights of mothers, wed or unwed, to economic consideration.[19]

In the first few chapters much space is given to sex education, but the chapter "Educación sexual" contains a more detailed analysis of its problems and offers some solutions but, for the present, Dr. Marin's main purpose is to emphasize the necessity of some kind of well-organized sex education. He points out the joint responsibility of the parents and the school, but he does not prepare a detailed plan of how this education is to be implemented.

Perhaps the most important section of *El problema* . . . is the chapter "El matrimonio controlado"—120 pages of the total of 375 in the entire book. Before explaining what he means by *matrimonio controlado,* Dr. Marin gives careful thought to what he considers to be the defects of Christian marriage and, although he is determined to maintain a position of tolerance, he criticizes the normal and almost universally held concept of matrimony—an institution misunderstood by many. The influence of St. Paul (Saul of Tarsus), who only tolerated marriage as the lesser of two evils, has been pernicious, for sex had come to be considered a sin unless its function was only for the purpose of procreation.

Substitutes for the traditional Christian marriage are discussed: trial marriage, companionate marriage, and even free love. Dr. Marin quotes a thesis held by several authors relating to the advantages and dangers faced by a man and a woman who are allowed to decide these things for themselves without the intervention of legal or religious institutions. He insists that the state's right to intervene in these very personal and intimate matters is permissible only in cases when a child is born to an extra-marital union. However, Dr. Marin himself believes in the monogamic marriage. But if in spite of all possible care in planning, both or either of the two parties to a union wish it, separation ought under certain very limited circumstances to be permitted.*

Because the bringing of children into the world must be considered along with marriage, Dr. Marin believes that the number of children in the family ought to be the decision of both parties to the union. Sexual continence is dismissed as a means of birth control. Sexual relations are to be considered an expression of love in its fullest sense and are, therefore, important for the continued physical and mental health of the couple.

Dr. Marin finally arrives at a careful analysis of what he calls "Matrimonio controlado" (Controlled Matrimony). His recapitulation and conclusions are likewise our summary: the monogamic union is the highest and the only acceptable one between man and woman; both parties ought to have a thorough and careful sex education; the marriage ought to be eugenic; birth control information should be easily available; abortion and sterilization are to be allowed under proper supervision, medical as well as legal; the trial or companionate marriage is not approved by Dr. Marin.

This notable book ends with a quotation from Jiménez Asúa. We translate:

> When in a future, who knows how distant, we discard
> the hobbles that link us to outgrown conventionalisms, the
> improvement of the (human) race will automatically be

---

* Dr. Marin did not favor easy divorce but like many other Chileans felt that some kind of legal separation ought to be recognized in his country.

achieved. And this will be not only in its physical and animal aspects, but also in its spiritual qualities.

Along with these perfect fountains of pure men and women, without ignorance or base prejudices, the ideal society will be serenely forged.[20]

ENSAYOS FREUDIANOS[21]

(Freudian Essays)

This collection of essays was published one year before Freud's death (which occurred in London in 1939) and, according to Dr. Marin's "Introduction," it encompasses Medical, Historical, and Artistic themes inspired by the philosophy of the Viennese Master.[22] Dr. Marin lays no claim to originality and declares that his work is, rather, an attempt to divulge some aspects of contemporary culture. The last sentence in his brief "Introduction" reveals the author's deep appreciation of Sigmund Freud: "May this book reach the Master's quiet retreat as a message of my fervent admiration."

Fittingly enough, the first chapter is a spiritual interpretation of Freud, whom Dr. Marin calls "the doctor Faustus of our times." It was read by the author in the Hall of Honor of the University of Chile, in May 1938, on the occasion of a public homage to Freud organized by the *Alianza de intelectuales de Chile.*

In the chapter "Génesis y proceso del arte" (Genesis and Process of Art),[23] Dr. Marin analyzes the process of artistic creation. What is art? Men always appear divided into two groups when attempting to explain it: the spiritualists and the materialists. There run through the two chapters, "Génesis y proceso del arte" and "Búsqueda de la dialéctica materialista a través del psicoanálisis freudiano," certain important conclusions reached by Dr. Marin: a) art cannot be treated as an isolated phenomenon, for it is a natural product of the society from which it emerges, b) attempts to create an *ivory tower type of art* are self-defeating, c) even the more sophisticated painters, sculptors, musicians, and men of letters, while insisting on "art for art's sake," seek, as did the primitive artists, to control their subjects by depicting them, d) the artist, although claiming to be realistic, i.e., to have no purpose other than to represent truthfully, cannot and ought not shun emotional involvement; absolute passivity, if it could be attained, would lead to indifference and indifference to insipidity. Hinted several times in Dr. Marin's creative writing is the accepted psychological thesis that the emotions of love and hatred, of egoism and altruism, although apparently opposites, are neighbors and may easily be reversed. Dr. Fraga's statement in the play *Orestes y yo*, "In my head are fighting the forces that move the world: love and hatred, beauty and crime, life and death . . . ," (See note 39 to Chapter III) indicates Dr. Marin's acceptance of the paradox of the juxtaposition of opposed emotions.

According to Dr. Marin, we are approaching a period in which humanity, to survive, must develop a new synthesis. He thinks that for Freud this synthesis probably meant an end to the perturbation arising in community life because of the human impulses of aggression and self-destruction. How? Possibly by the arrival of a collective Super Ego akin to the Super Ego acting within the individual conscience.[24]

"Restif de la Bretonne o el fetichismo del pie"[25] is a psychoanalytic study of a writer, a man famous in his day but now forgotten unless remembered for his vices and for the morbid nature of his personality. Leading French psychiatrists have studied this personality, coming to the conclusion that Restif was a typical case of polymorphic sexual perversion developing on a psychopathic, paranoic background. Restif's major sexual perversion was fetichism of the foot. This particular fetichism flourished in the magic period of human culture when the limit between the imaginary and the real seemed very indefinite and confusing. Sexual fetichism is an example of that animistic phase in the development of man. Here the libido is fixed to primitive, archaic stages of cultural evolution.

Restif was a prolific writer; his last work, *Monsieur Nicolas,* is an autobiography in sixteen volumes. His books will no doubt be used as true clinical records by future psychologists when investigating the origin and evolution of sexual perversions.

In his chapter on Paul Gauguin, Dr. Marin vividly describes the exquisite torture that creation entails for some artists, a semblance of satanic possession, an unceasing effort to bring to light the inner fruits of creation. Gauguin would have been submerged in a sterile neurosis had his psyche not blossomed in a blaze of genius.

A curious and interesting situation developed from the attitude of Tolstoy toward medicine, writes Dr. Marin in the chapter "Disección psicoanalítica de León Tolstoy" (Psychoanalytic Dissection of Leon Tolstoy). Throughout his life Tolstoy never missed an opportunity to revile and to belittle doctors and medicine. When his wife became seriously ill, he sternly prohibited an operation that might have saved her life. But this apostle of peace and brotherly love, while constantly condemning the carnal act as a curse, ignored the increasing danger of child bearing to his wife's health and proceeded to engender eight more children.[26]

B. Eikelbaum points out in an excellent study that history has pictured Tolstoy as a grand old Count-mujik, white bearded, barefooted, and bloused in coarse cloth.[27] One tends to forget the noble military man of licentious habits, the cruel landowner who brutally lashed his serfs. Studied in the light of psychoanalysis by N. Nazinova, doctor Dégline, and especially by Nina Gourfinkel, Tolstoy is seen as a man who suffered from anxiety neurosis, an invincible dread of death, nervous crises, sensuality, cruelty, and megalomania.[28]

In the chapter "Habría descubierto la medicina las localizaciones del inconsciente freudiano?" (Has medicine discovered— or is it on the point of discovering—the location of the Freudian unconscious?), Dr. Marin states that ever since man has existed his thirst for knowledge has led him to inquire in what part of the body is housed the blaze of conscious life? Where sojourns the personal Ego, unique and unconfounded? Our author thinks that the enigma of the mind-matter relation is in the process of being solved and that present investigations in the field of neurology concerning vegetative, subcortical, and hormonal life are of enormous importance.

"Descartes y el alma humana" (Descartes and the Human Soul) is a chapter that studies the mistakes committed by the philosopher-mathematician, Descartes, through over-simplification in his search for truth. He tentatively places the human soul in the pineal gland though he never performed any anatomic investigation to prove his point and, when drawing his conclusions, forgot his own dictum, "Never accept as true a thing that is not evidently known as such."

Dr. Marin reminds us that, when Descartes published his conception of "The Machine and the Machinist" (The Body and the Soul), it had already been nine years since Harvey discovered the circulation of the blood in 1628. Descartes, the founder of the experimental method, the philosopher of objective reasoning, is the author of the most formidable speculation. No one, since Galen and Aristotle, has caused a greater upheaval in the fields of biology and medicine, says Dr. Marin.

Queen Christina of Sweden passes through the political history of Europe as a yet unsolved enigma, wrote Dr. Marin in "Cristina de Suecia, la reina intersexual" (Christina of Sweden, the Intersexual Queen). She has been considered mad or hypocritical by some, degenerate or vicious by others. When she was born she was thought to be a boy. Was it a mal-conformation of her organs, that is, was she really intersexual? Her reluctance to marry, her hatred of women, the mystery with which she always performed her intimate toilet, and some of the expressions found in her memoirs lend support to continuing doubts concerning her sexuality. In the psychical as in the physical spheres, she was intersexual. In spite of a tendency to lesbianism, she also had many male lovers.

In Christina the psychological determinants coincide, according to Dr. Marin, with the endocrine factors together with the background of a degenerative heritage. Her infantile libido fixed on her father by identification, her bitter experiences in heterosexual love and her profound inferiority complex made her a sexual pervert, an anti-social element, frivolous, capricious, deceptive, and spectacular.

In "Byron y el incesto" (Byron and Incest), Dr. Marin claims priority in explaining and naming incest between brother and sister "El complejo de Byron" (The Byron Complex). This physical attraction is a substitute for the Oedipus complex, i.e., the brother substituting a sister for the mother and the girl substituting her brother for the father. From the beginning of time, incest has been condemned and vigorously repressed by society. Many primitive tribes prohibit endogamy as an additional deterrent to incest. Byron's character was further complicated by an inferiority complex, due to a lameness that he fought to disguise. His sexual perversion included narcissism because, except for his deformity, he was considered the handsomest of men.

In the chapter "Emoción y neurosis" (Emotion and Neurosis), one of the most scientific sections of Dr. Marin's book, he calls attention to the increase in the twenty years (1918-1938) of those disturbances of the mind called neuroses. These processes, a labor not yet finished, have been identified and classified thanks to the explorations begun by Freud.

The present panorama of human society is confusing. There is a profound collective anxiety expressing the sum of individual anxieties and this is reflected in all the diverse activities of man on earth. Art, literature, technology, and even science are advancing in gigantic but halting steps, falling at times into the void, then recovering and advancing, always in an absurd and incomprehensible world.

Man is engaged not merely in a fight to the death for the conquest of his own well-being but he also tries to solve the riddles of nature hoping to use the still uncontrolled elements for his own benefit. This thrilling struggle of man with the cosmos commenced some centuries ago, but only now has entered its more acute and decisive stage. The human organism suffers the most violent stresses under these new conditions. Still it must adapt in order to survive. Even science is forced to alternate with sports and in many ways both activities seem to coalesce in some of their maximum aspirations, such as interplanetary travel, exploration of the depths of the sea, and in other ways. Man might have been the conductor and guide of the machine for the greater benefit of the community. Unfortunately it is not always true, and the machine has become the tool of the aggressive tendencies existing in the human psyche.

The last essay, which seems to have been one of Dr. Marin's lectures while he was professor of the History of Medicine, makes no mention of Freud but is quite intriguing for it seems to be positive proof that the Spaniards did not bring syphilis from the New World to Europe but that, quite to the contrary, they introduced it into America by way of the island now occupied by the Dominican Republic and Haiti. While Dr. Marin does not declare categorically that syphilis was brought to the New World by the Spanish *conquistadores,* his arguments appear quite convincing. The chapter ends on an optimistic note as Dr. Marin predicts an early eradication of this so-called social disease.

In our discussions of Dr. Marin's medical publications, four volumes beginning with the rather simple and factual compositions of *Clínicas* . . . and ending with the much more technical and, at times, abstruse presentation of theories and conclusions of *Ensayos freudianos,* one notes the gradual maturing of style and a move from the down-to-earth essays of the first books to the more philosophical generalizations of the latter. As in his poetry and again in his prose fiction, one notes the ripening of the writer and of the philosopher. With no attempt or desire to depreciate *Clínicas* . . . , *Poliedro* . . . , or *El problema* . . . , we cannot fail to consider *Ensayos freudianos* the culmination of our author's medical and psychological writings. Several of the essays of this collection are seriously studied by experts in their fields. For example *Génesis y proceso del arte* was published in *Atenea* and listed in the *Bibliography* of *La evolución de la crítica literaria en Chile* by Professor John P. Dyson.[29] References are often made to other essays published in *Ensayos freudianos*.

From time to time in the course of this study we have had occasion to call attention to the struggle faced by Juan Marin, the man of medical science and Juan Marin, the creative writer. As late as 1952, when he resigned from the diplomatic corps, he considered returning to a civilian practice of surgery. Being a very conscientious person, however, he felt that a return to surgery would require several months of refresher courses in some medical school; so many new discoveries and improved techniques called for a period of intensive review of courses he had followed in medical school days and initiation into new ones. Many of his friends, however, advised that he return to medicine; his training had been excellent; his grades in medical school outstanding, and his reputation during his years of practice enviable. We have been told, also, that while he was giving his time to diplomacy and consular duties he had kept in close touch with medical societies and doctors: in China, in Egypt, and in India. Doctors and medicine are often mentioned in his non-medical writings.

When the Marins returned to Chile Dr. Marin was relatively young, 52 years of age. Many stories are told that show that he had not dismissed entirely the possibility of renewing medical practice. He often visited friends and when one of these was incapacitated by sickness, either in a hospital or at home, his visits took on a semi-professional character. For example he visited his long time friend don Enrique Molina who in his mid-eighties was finally indisposed. He also visited Luis Durand, author of *Fronteras* who had almost lost his already failing eye-sight and was seriously ill. In both cases Dr. Marin examined and questioned these men and consoled them with optimistic prognostications.

We are convinced that Dr. Marin could have remade a very

successful career in medicine and surgery, but fortunately other opportunities outside of medicine presented themselves. But even as Director of the Office of Cultural Affairs for the OAS he did not lose his interest in the advances in medical sciences. The book-length publications mentioned in this chapter will be valuable reference works in medical schools for years to come.

CHAPTER VII

Juan Marin, Critic

Although Juan Marin shows the depth of vision and the understanding of the professional critic, he was primarily a creative writer. The time and energy he devoted to judging the literary works of others were grudgingly stolen from the hours that, we are convinced, he would have preferred to spend finishing some of the novels that he had planned. But his own extensive and careful literary preparation gave to his critical writings such ready acceptance that all too much of the last period of his life (1956-1963), after his appointment to the position of Director of the Department of Cultural Affairs of the Organization of American States, was devoted to articles concerning other men of letters. At the same time he was continually publishing essays on medicine and on contemporary events.

We had anticipated spending days working through miscellaneous newspaper files while carrying on our investigations, but we were pleasantly surprised to discover that Doña Milena Luksic de Marin had, in addition to duplicate copies of all of her husband's works, dozens of notebooks filled with clippings, including hundreds of his critical essays, carefully classified and dated with the name of the newspaper or magazine that had first published them. Dr. Marin usually offered his articles to the *Mercurio de Santiago* but other publications were not slighted.* There are to be found in Doña Milena's home in the cozy room that was the study of her late husband hundreds of book reviews and articles of literary criticism, some of them as early as 1922. The earlier ones do not show the same maturity of judgment as those written between 1956 and 1963.

---

* In one section of our *Bibliographies* there are listed the principal magazines and newspapers, both Chilean and international, that published Dr. Marin's shorter articles.

We know that Dr. Marin was a very well-read man and that his personal library was extensive, mainly in the Spanish, English, and French languages. Doña Milena has been most generous with gifts from her husband's collection to the Columbus Memorial Library, the library of the Instituto de Investigaciones de Literatura Chilena, the Biblioteca Nacional de Chile, and the Library of Congress.

From these notebooks of clippings and the several hundred articles that we were privileged to examine while preparing this chapter on Dr. Marin as a critic, we have selected eight essays as typical of his literary acumen. Many of his critical essays deal with North American authors but he also discusses French, Italian, Russian, and English writers—and even some of the outstanding poets of the Far East.

For our purposes we discuss the following as examples of his critical ideas: Rousseau, Thoreau, Upton Sinclair, Faulkner, Hemingway, Steinbeck and Pasternak, as well as a general brief essay on the state of poetry in the United States.

Juan Jacobo Rousseau

This essay was written on the occasion of the 250th anniversary of the birth of the author of *Confessions*. After a short resumé of Rousseau's life and writings, Dr. Marin ends by saying, "Today Rousseau's influence is quite reduced, but it is evident that his ideas exercised a terrible and incalculable influence on the men of the French Revolution."[1]

H. D. Thoreau

Juan Marin always recognized the value and necessity of discipline and conformity; however, he expressed in his article on Thoreau his admiration for the rebel, but a rebel with a program. In this criticism Dr. Marin finds the essence of Rousseau and Thoreau to be a philosophical reinterpretation of democracy and civilization as we are beginning to understand them. As a well educated man with inborn and developed qualities that make for a great diplomat, Dr. Marin believed that most of us can make our greatest contribution without rebelling against society, but he realized at the same time that spirits such as Thoreau are needed. Juan Marin himself could and did speak out without fear of retribution when he deemed it was the right time to do so. This article, written on the occasion of the 100th anniversary of the death of the *Hermit of Walden,* brings out his sympathy for the rebel.[2]

Upton Sinclair

Dr. Marin apparently had read the works of Upton Sinclair soon after they were published in Spanish. In spite of saying in his essay that North Americans have almost forgotten our novelist Upton Sinclair, Dr. Marin continued to consider him to be one of our truly great spirits. It is an essay written in 1961 when on Sinclair's 83rd birthday a special celebration was organized in his honor. This short criticism, published under the general heading of "Día a día" (Day by Day), is one of the most revealing that we have read. Dr. Marin himself shows the same compassion for the down-and-outer in *Viento negro* and *Paralelo 53 sur* that Upton Sinclair evidenced in his extremely socialistic novels.[3]

Faulkner

After having read several hundred pages of Dr. Marin's essays, many of them very penetrating, we have come to the opinion that the one dealing with Faulkner is among the most discerning, second only to his several on Hemingway. We permit ourselves to insert a personal note. We were visiting Dr. Marin in his beautiful office in one of the Pan-American buildings and happened to mention Faulkner's latest book, *The Reivers,* a novel that we had glanced at superficially. Having had our own difficulties with some of Faulkner's earlier works, we asked Dr. Marin, "Do you not find some obscurity in a few of Faulkner's novels, for example, *As I Lay Dying* or *A Light in August?*" His answer did not come immediately. After a few seconds of deep thought he replied, "For one who has not lived in Jefferson (Oxford, Mississippi) and does not know the people of the middle or lower classes, there are some puzzling sentences."

In his essay on Faulkner he makes the following statement, "One would say that Faulkner in his sinuous caprices takes pleasure in strewing thorns in the path of the reader. . . ."[4]

He went on to ask us certain questions, mainly having to do with the relationship of White and Black people, questions that proved that he understood Faulkner better than many people who have lived some of the experiences described in *Intruder in the Dust* or *The Mansion*. One notices with surprise the exact and thorough knowledge Juan Marin had of English, including its usage in the United States. He easily recognized the peculiarities of Faulkner's choice of words and his sometimes unwieldy sentences.

After pointing out the strong and weak features of Faulkner's compositions, Dr. Marin asks and answers an interesting question:

> With this immense ballast (i.e. Faulkner's puzzling style) what then are the virtues that make of Faulkner the most widely read, the most translated, and the most imitated author?[5]

His answer to this question is concise but in part, at least, correct. "The reason for Faulkner's great popularity is his use of southern themes . . . the vigor in the telling of the story. . . ."[6]

The critic who must, in a very few pages or even in a few sentences, discover a writer's strengths and weaknesses, cannot be slowed down by details; he will see immediately the essence of the writer's style or message and express it laconically.

Hemingway

Among the critical essays that we have chosen for analysis, those dealing with Hemingway are without doubt the most significant. We feel that unusual warmth and enthusiasm are justified when they do not militate against the objectivity that the critic is supposed to maintain. Hemingway is described as a man of action, a man who would have preferred to live his novels rather than to write them. One finds in the brief remarks about Hemingway, besides critical insight, creative writing as beautiful as any found in *Paralelo* . . . or *Viento negro*. It will be evident in the following selection that the lyrical element does not lessen its value:

> "Never ask for whom the bells toll; they toll for you."
> This, Ernest Hemingway wrote in the prologue of his dramatic and widely read novel *For Whom the Bell Tolls*. Today, while we are writing these lines, the bells of the little church of Sun Valley, Idaho are tolling. . . .

And again in the last paragraph of the essay, "Hemingway has ended it all on the morning of July 3, 1961 in his little country house among the high mountains of Idaho."[7]

Throughout this essay, Juan Marin insists that Hemingway must be judged by all of his writings and not, as some apparently prefer, by his last novel *The Old Man and the Sea*. Even *Across the River and Into the Trees* (Scorned or damned by slight praise) is given a place of honor by Dr. Marin. Later he indicates some of Hemingway's peculiarities of style.[8]

Steinbeck

Dr. Marin's essay on Steinbeck on the occasion of his receiving the Nobel Prize for Literature brings forth a very illuminating remark that shows how interested our author was in the novel of social impact, a phase of his own writings emphasized in *Viento negro* as well as in several of his short stories. He goes on to list the great American novelists who have been awarded the Nobel Prize for Literature: Sinclair Lewis, Pearl Buck, Hemingway, and others saying:

> It is curious to note that all of these, to a greater or lesser degree, have in their writings a nonconformity, a breath of rebellion, and a strong trend toward social criticism.[9]

157

It is clear that Juan Marin had read carefully most of Steinbeck, even *Travels With Charlie* which, although not a novel in the usually accepted sense, has had a certain popularity. Dr. Marin felt that the awarding of the Nobel Prize to Steinbeck was long overdue. Steinbeck's sympathy for the under dog and his struggle to do something about social injustices did not, in our author's eyes, detract from his literary excellence.[10] In his remarks on Steinbeck, he makes reference to the humor that softens the tragedy recorded in his novels of sociological trend.

Pasternak

The death of Boris Pasternak caused to be published, over the entire civilized world, articles that for the most part refer to the inhuman treatment accorded by the Russians to their great writer. Dr. Marin's essay "Boris Pasternak" calls the author of *Doctor Zhivago* an addition to the great trilogy of Russian novelists— Tolstoy, Dostoevsky, and Turgenev. He quotes a famous statement by Pasternak that bares the great Russian writer's soul, "I have wished to show life just as it is, within its intimate nature." Pasternak had never wanted his novel to become a political pamphlet; even less could he dream that it would be transformed into one of the most polemic works of this century.[11]

Juan Marin quotes from one of Pasternak's poems (probably his own translation), a poem that reveals the mental and spiritual suffering of the Russian. We paraphrase a few lines in English:

> . . . But what evil thing have I done,
> What crime have I committed,
> I who am called assassin and villain?
> I whose only crime is to have made the whole world
> Weep at the beauties of my land?[12]

At the end of this essay Dr. Marin pays Pasternak the greatest of all tributes:

> His book has been read by millions of human beings
> who have found in it art and emotion, and especially a

large dose of poetry, of that authentic poetry which is like
the breath of earth, like the respiration of man's soul.
Pasternak did better than he realized. In his book, *Doctor
Zhivago,* he crossed the frontiers of Russia and became a
part of the spiritual baggage of all humanity.[13]

ESSAY ON AMERICAN POETRY

We end this chapter concerning Dr. Marin's critical writings
with his short comment on poetry in general and North American
poets in particular. He begins, "Some will ask the question, 'Why
talk about poetry when the world is on the verge of being de-
stroyed by the "A" or the "H" bomb!' " His answer indicates that
he believed that poetry is always needed, "Because," he said, "if
the end of the world is to come from the "A" or the "H" bomb,
the best thing that could happen is that it find us reciting or
listening to poetry."[14]

Juan Marin was a great admirer of Whitman and Poe but was
left unmoved by some poets that we consider superior, Sandburg
or Frost, for example. Finding so much to admire and enjoy in
our great contemporary novels and dramas, he could not explain
why our contemporary poetry is so lacking in force. "There is
no parallel," he writes, "between the vigor of the novel and the
drama in the United States and the anemic figure shown by
poetry."[15]

Although there are notable exceptions, it is often said that a
creative writer is seldom a great critic; the converse, that seldom
is a great critic an outstanding creative writer, is just as true.
There are, however, in Dr. Marin's critical opinions expressed
in the brief essays discussed in Chapter VII as well as in a chapter of *Ensayos freudianos,* "Génesis y proceso del arte," also published in *Atenea,* important statements by Juan Marin that are
most revealing. Perhaps the most significant are those that insist on the importance of the imagination, the contributions made
to realistic writing by psychological, spiritual, and extrasensorial
values. The accepted five senses may well be reinforced by in-

tuition, telepathy, and other extrasensory communication. Even spiritism may contribute to the poet's inspiration.

In conclusion we should like to reiterate that Dr. Marin, in spite of his excellent qualities as a critic, was primarily a creative writer.

CHAPTER VIII

Juan Marin, the Man and the Writer

In chapters II through VII the varied categories of writings by Juan Marin have been presented. While discussing the compositions under each heading, one title has merited more praise than others; the decision as to which is superior has been difficult in many cases. In this Chapter VIII is found a recapitulation, listing the six works given preference and the one item of all of Dr. Marin's extensive literary production that we consider his masterpiece.

JUAN MARIN—THE WRITER

Poetry

From his several poems worthy of note, we have selected "Mecánica" published in *Aquarium*. "Mecánica" besides representing Juan Marin's mature style serves as a manifesto, a declaration of the poet's right to broaden the field of subjects. One almost regrets having decided on one single item in each category for "Atlantic cabaret," in some ways, appeals more to one's sentiments. Likewise the shorter poems, for example "Sinfonía blanca," demonstrate the poet's ability to produce pure poetry, poetry with no purpose except that of emphasizing the music of words.

Short Stories

Of the twenty-six short stories presented in Section I of Chapter III there are extremes of realism and fantasy. The fantastic element, not only in his short stories but in his other writings, will continue to interest the student of Juan Marin. In spite of the artistic use of extrasensory perception, which includes telepathy, spiritism, and other non-materialistic spheres, we choose the very realistic *cuento,* "Puerto negro," from the collection *Cuentos de viento y agua.* "Puerto negro" is long enough to allow the author to use his exceptional descriptive powers but short enough to keep the unity that a good short story needs.

Novelettes and Novels

In Section II, *Novelettes,* and Section III, *Novels,* one finds frequent mention of *Paralelo 53 sur, Orestes y yo,* and *Viento negro* as examples of Juan Marin's fictional art at its high point. The first has had many editions and deserves its wide acclaim; the second is often dismissed as being "only a psychological study"; and as for the third, a growing list of critics is beginning to give it preference. Because of its masterly character delineation, its carefully chosen and relevant descriptions, and its logically developed and powerful, tragic plot, all bound together by an inescapable unity of interaction of events, we differ from the almost unanimous choice of the Chilean public and professional critics who prefer *Paralelo 53 sur* to nominate, as Dr. Marin's greatest novel, *Viento negro.*

Philosophies, Religions, and Civilizations

With little vacillation *Mesa de mah-jong* is given first place in this category, although one is tempted to establish a separate division for religions in order to honor *Buda o la negación del mundo* which has some of Dr. Marin's superior writing and a sympathetic insight into Far Eastern religious thought. *Mesa de mah-jong* is chosen over its companion piece *Alma de China* because it has more of poetry, more of the author, and less factual reporting.

Travel and Interpretation

In this section there are presented Dr. Marin's interpretations of two great civilizations. *La India eterna,* depending more on the present than *El Egipto de los faraones,* provides the author with greater opportunities to show that contemporary humanity is more interesting to him than the past, even though he has mingled with his reconstruction of ancient Egyptian history much of poetry and human interest. In *La India eterna* Dr. Marin is philosophically and intellectually at home in the land of Mahatma Gandhi and Tagore not to mention Buddha and Krishna. *La India eterna* therefore is our choice from this classification.

Medical Writings

With only momentary hesitation we choose, from the several books on medical subjects, *Ensayos freudianos.* In spite of the variety of matter treated in this volume, there is always the unifying core built around the great Viennese psychologist. Even in the essay dealing with the origin and evolution of art, "Genesis y proceso del arte," Freud's psychology is kept prominent.

Critical Essays

Dr. Marin's critical acumen is most evident in his discussions of North American novelists of his own generation, the writers who were beginning to make literary history in the Twenties: Faulkner, Hemingway, and Steinbeck. His views of these three are penetrating but his opinions of Hemingway show a judicious mingling of thorough knowledge of the novelist's works and a humanitarian appreciation of the man. The essay written immediately after Hemingway's death is our choice.

THE ONE BOOK

As with other writers, Juan Marin will eventually be known for one book; for this honor we suggest *Viento negro.*

JUAN MARIN—THE MAN

Chapter I of this study dealt with the story of the life of Juan Marin, pointing out, among other things, personal character traits.

Although we realize that his characteristics and his writings cannot be separated, we devote a few lines to *Juan Marin—the Man* but shall have to make reference to his works while doing this.

An important characteristic of Dr. Marin was his liberality of thought and his sympathy for the credos of the religions of the world, as well as his determination to learn more about them. He was fortunate to have a home environment that helped him maintain a firm balance as a freethinker: his father's well-known liberalism and his mother's acceptance of the teachings of the Roman Catholic church. Juan arrived at the Liceo de Talca in 1910, when he was only ten years of age, to find two of his teachers struggling against religious intolerance and obscurantism. These two, Enrique Molina and Alejandro Venegas, ecouraged their students to maintain an open and inquiring stance toward religions and philosophies. Juan's four years in the Liceo de Talca (1910-1914) strengthened his liberal attitude in regard to religious thought.

Nearly all who have written about Juan Marin have emphasized his *inquietud intelectual* (intellectual curiosity). One guesses from the many references to great intellectuals in his short stories, novels, and essays that his reading in the Talca secondary school was wide and varied. Previously it has been noted that he insisted on learning to fly a plane, that in medical school he interested himself much more in the workings of the human mind than required by general medical studies and that in China, India, El Salvador, and Egypt he went to extremes to document himself on the geography, history, and civilization of these four countries.

Stories have been told to prove Dr. Marin's physical courage, but we are more interested in his mental and spiritual fearlessness. As an experienced naval officer and diplomat, he realized the importance of discipline and conformity. Nevertheless when convinced that certain beliefs and acts were essential for the progress of society or for relieving suffering, he expressed himself and acted in spite of the consequences. His championing of family planning, sex education, and emancipation of woman is evident in several of his writings, noticeably in *El problema sexual y sus nuevas fórmulas sociales.*

Dr. Marin did not give the impression that he was a sentimentalist; however, his sympathy for the down-and-outer, for the weak and helpless, especially for women and children, is constantly present in his poems, his short stories, and his novels as well as in his essays.

Loyalty was a quality greatly esteemed by Dr. Marin. In such short stories as "El 'curco' Meléndez," in the novels *Margarita, el aviador y el médico, Un avión volaba,* and *Viento negro* there is noted his impatience with persons guilty of double-dealings.

Frequently in the course of this study one may note the recurring theme—that the imagination, the non-materialistic, and the idealistic are of prime importance to Juan Marin. In this respect he makes frequent use of the extrasensory, including telepathy and spiritualism. His short stories classified as fantastic attest to his discarding of the purely materialistic.

Any person whose experiences endow him with cosmopolitanism is often unjustly classified as unpatriotic. The true patriot may see and experience things in foreign countries that could be of benefit to his own homeland. This does not, for that reason, make him less patriotic. Dr. Marin always maintained a deep-seated love for Chile. Dr. José A. Balseiro even suggested in his criticism of the last pages of *Paralelo 53 sur* that its *chilenidad* may have militated against the artistic qualities of the last incident of this great novel. We remember the pride with which Dr. Marin spoke of such fellow Chileans as Gabriela Mistral, Pablo Neruda, and of Eduardo Barrios, to mention only literary figures. Chile, so it seems to many students of that country, is the least provincial of the Spanish American republics. Juan Marin like others of his compatriots (Salvador Reyes, Edwards Bello, and Blest Gana) was a citizen of the world and also essentially Chilean.

It would be possible to point out other interesting personal characteristics of Juan Marin, but in summary the following are the most important: liberality in religion, intellectual curiosity, moral courage, compassion, loyalty, imaginativeness, idealism, cosmopolitanism, and patriotism.

Juan Marin, during the course of his varied and intense life, was a questing spirit in constant ferment, leaving traces of his ardors as surgeon, aviator, poet, literary critic, journalist, diplomat and international functionary. But undoubtedly where his fame rests is as a writer. His vast culture permitted him to lose himself in the mysteries, rites, and symbols of ancient civilizations which fructified in his books on China, India, and Egypt. The life of this talented man, oriented from his youth to the service of mankind with the devotion and sincerity that stamp all his actions, should be a living example to all people. He will be remembered as a leader in the vanguard of his generation.

General Notes

Chapter 1

1. Osvaldo Paez Bogginni. *La novela de la generación actual.* (Para optar el título de Profesor de Estado en la Asignatura de Castellano.) Instituto Pedagógico, Valparaíso: 1962.

2. See *El mar en la literatura chilena.* Manuel Montecinos. Editorial del Pacífico, Santiago: 1956. 244 pages. (pp. 135-156 discuss Dr. Marin as a writer of the sea.)

3. We list those that we know personally: Arturo Torres-Rioseco, Francisco Aguilera, Eduardo Neale-Silva, Juan Lovelock, Fernando Alegría, and Homero Castillo, all of whom have contributed more than a little to the educational and cultural achievements of the United States.

4. First given to Augusto Thompson (Augusto d'Halmar) in 1942.

5. Even in the trade magazine published by the Chilean National Railways, *En viaje,* much space is given to cultural matters including literature.

6. The sources for this Biography are: *Who's Who in Latin America,* Third Edition, Vol. IV; hours of talks with Dr. Marin himself; almost daily visits with Doña Milena during the summers of 1965 and 1968; conversations with many fellow medical students of Juan invited to luncheons, teas, or dinners at Doña Milena's residence and chats with other persons who knew Dr. Marin well.

7. In the catalogue of the Library of Congress, for example, our author's birth date was listed as 1897 but in the revision being completed at this moment (1971) the change to 1900 is being made.

8. For more information concerning this remarkable philosopher-educator see: Armando Bazán, *Vida y obra del maestro Enrique Molina.* Nascimento, Santiago: 1954, 160 pages.

9. Published in *Alas sobre el mar,* page 165, 1934 but dated 1926.

10. *Looping,* p. 4ff.

10a. *Op. cit.,* p. 73.

11. *"El Mercurio"* (Unless otherwise designated *El Mercurio* will mean the Santiago, Chile publication) September 6, 1932.

12. A dissertation required at that time of all candidates for the M.D. degree. In 1958 this requirement was abolished.

13. When Aviation was separated into a new military establishment, Dr. Marin chose to transfer to the Navy but never lost his interest in flying.

14. *Op. cit.*, p. 5 ff.

15. *Poliedro médico*, pages 83-95. Also published as a reprint with the title of *El origen de la medicina hipocrática* (see Bibliography).

16. *Clínicas y maestros en Inglaterra y Francia* (1931), *Margarita, el aviador y el médico* (1932), *La muerte de Julián Aranda* (1933), *Alas sobre el mar* (1934), *Aquarium* (1934), *Hacia la nueva moral* (1934), *Un avión volaba* (1935), *Paralelo 53 sur* (1936), *El secreto del Dr. Baloux* (1936), *El problema sexual* (1937), *Ensayos freudianos* (1938), *Naufragio* (1939), and *Orestes y yo* (1939).

17. For example, *El Egipto de los faraones* has 380 pages and *La India eterna* 475.

18. This book, *China*, was published in three separate studies of the three great religio-philosophical leaders: *Lao-Tszé. . . . , Confucio . . . ,* and *Buda. . . .* (See Chapter IV for a discussion of these.)

19. *Congressional Record.* Vol. 109, March 9, 1963. No. 36, p. 3529.

20. *El diario latino* famous newspaper of San Salvador, El Salvador.

21. Posthumous publication in the Sunday Literary section of *El Mercurio*, March 22, 1964 and in *La Opinión*, Los Angeles, California: May 10, 1964.

22. *Muerte en Shanghai.* Editorial Rollán (Madrid: 1953), 93 pages. (This is a very exciting novel based on the murder of a Chinese quisling.)

23. "Instituto Internacional de Literatura Iberoamericana" usually designated simply with the letters IILI.

24. Fernando Alegría's first fame came with the publication of his prize winning novel *Lautaro.* One of his better, more recent novels, translated to French and English, *Caballo de copas,* has its setting in California.

25. James O. Swain. *Prólogo* to a study by Marilyn Landers-Terry, *The Prose Fiction of Juan Marin.* (Graphic Arts, University of Tennessee) 1964, 74 pages.

26. These books will be discussed in following chapters of this study.

27. See Chapter VII "Juan Marin—Critic" of this study.

28. *Palabras del Dr. José A. Mora, Secretario General de la OEA (OAS) en ocasión del Homenaje ofrecido a la memoria del doctor Juan Marín. Día 20 de marzo de 1963 en la Unión Panamericana.*

HOMENAJE AL DOCTOR JUAN MARIN

Estamos esta noche reunidos en el Salón de las Américas para rendir homenaje a la memoria de un ilustre hijo de Chile que se destacó en muy diversos aspectos de la Cultura, de las Letras y de las Ciencias Médicas y en quien se cumplió la clásica sentencia: "Nada de lo humano me es ajeno."

El doctor Juan Marín, fué hombre americano por vocación y universal por sus conocimientos. Su recuerdo habrá de perdurar para siempre como el de un espíritu que impulsó todos los ideales que unen a los pueblos de América.

En sus funciones de Director del Departamento de Asuntos Culturales de la Secretaría General de la OEA, o como Presidente del Ateneo Americano de Washington, mantuvo siempre despierta una acción desinteresada para enaltecer los valores más altos y representativos de nuestro Continente.

Al ingresar en esta Casa, después de haber ejercido actividades en la Medicina y en la Diplomacia, áreas aparentemente tan dispares, supo iniciar una nueva era en su vida de hombre enamorado del Humanismo. Luchó ahincadamente por romper las vallas que se oponen a las comunicaciones entre las mentes de los hombres de América. Con frase feliz decía que las culturas americanas se mantienen obstinadamente alejadas unas de otras, como islas de un vasto archipiélago. Todos sus esfuerzos se encaminaron, por lo tanto, a convertir ese archipiélago en un continente, en una tierra firme. Trató de eliminar las dos más obstinadas barreras que se oponen al acercamiento cultural: La incomprensión entre las varias culturas, por una parte, y el desnivel entre las capas sociales de una misma cultura, por la otra.

Todos nosotros sabemos lo mucho que él hizo para lograr los dos objetivos fundamentales de la cooperación intelectual, en los distintos campos culturales: educación, filosofía y letras, música y artes plásticas, bibliografía y biblioteconomía. Para él la cultura fué siempre un concepto integral, un todo orgánico en que el equilibrio de las partes o funciones es elemento básico para lograr el armonioso desarrollo del conjunto. En uno de sus últimos artículos comentó, con su acostumbrada penetración, la división del mundo en dos sectores: el de los que saben y el de los que no saben; a estos últimos los estimó en las dos-quintas partes de la población del globo y creo que, en ello se quedó corto. Destacó la urgencia en iluminar ese mundo "en sombras." Consideró además a la cultura como un concepto esencialmente democrático: para él no bastaba con acercar los unos a los otros, los que no saben a los que ya saben, sino que consideraba indispensable proporcionar a los que no saben la oportunidad de llegar a saber, a fin de incorporarse rápidamente al proceso de una efectiva comunicación humana.

Al fomentar las distintas formas de la cultura, propugnó también en favor de la libertad. Tenía la convicción profunda de que la característica primordial de América es su identificación con el concepto de la libertad. Las interpretaciones materialistas y la filosofía dialéctica de la historia no encontraron acogida en su espíritu generoso: para él la superestructura, la creación superior, no podría derivar de lo inferior, ni los elementos materiales podrían ser causa de los valores espirituales. Por eso, dijo con acierto: "Nosotros pensamos que, en la base de todo fenómeno social, hay siempre un elemento cultural. Lo esencial es que en los problemas que afectan al hombre y a la sociedad humana exista siempre un hecho cultural. Detrás de una máquina, de una herramienta, de un instrumento, debe, necesariamente, existir una idea, una intuición, un razonamiento, una fuerza, en resumen: un elemento espiritual. Y como ozono vivificante un soplo robusto de libertad."

A los valores eternos del espíritu la libertad y la democracia consagró Marin integralmente su vida hasta el último aliento cuando cayó luchando por la integración de nuestra América. Posiblemente fué la muerte que él buscó al servicio de una idea-fuerza como él sabía y había logrado concebirla.

Juan Marín ostentaba los rasgos enérgicos de su nacionalidad chilena derivados, al parecer, de una geografía austera, entre mares y montañas, que provoca una recia aptitud, en un constante esfuerzo viril que no admite condescendencias para vencer a la naturaleza. En los años en que tuve el privilegio de gozar de su amistad aprendí a conocer al hombre, al hombre de principios e ideales que fué Juan Marín. Su personalidad debemos definirla como ejemplo de amigo y como ejemplo de lealtad, virtudes difíciles, con las que el ser humano se emancipa de toda servidumbre de la materia para realizarse en las esencias, donde sentimos la presencia de Dios.

Al ofrecerle este sencillo acto recordatorio lo hacemos con nostalgia y admiración.

Está a nuestro lado la compañera de sus esfuerzos, de sus sueños y de sus sufrimientos, doña Milena Luksic de Marín. En su personalidad fuerte de mujer sabemos que seguirá presente Juan Marín y al rendir un sincero homenaje al escritor, al colaborador sobresaliente, al amigo entrañable y, más aún, al hombre en la plenitud del vocablo, queremos fortalecer los ideales que con él compartimos y que seguiremos defendiendo como él lo hizo.

El navegante infatigable que se formó en las rudas jornadas de los mares del Sur de Chile, enamorado de todos los horizontes, que siguió los pasos de las culturas de oriente a occidente, emprendió ahora el gran viaje hacia lo desconocido, abandonándonos a la orilla del océano misterioso. Pero su ejemplo y su obra seguirán iluminando a las presentes y futuras generaciones de América.

29. At the same session the late Muna Lee spoke to the topic:

Juan Marin: His Work as Americanist

Remarks by Muna Lee
Cultural Liason Officer, Public Affairs Staff

Bureau of Inter-American Affairs, Department of State.

Because Muna Lee spoke in English we do not give her words in Spanish translation. We do, however, feel that a resumé in Spanish ought to be included in these NOTES:

El tema de la Señora Muna Lee fue la labor del Dr. Marín como Americanista, palabra ésta que aún no está bien definida, —explicó ella— pero que en lo que a él concernía, las definiciones más amplias no son las suficientes para describirlo.

Como Director del Departamento de Asuntos Culturales de la Unión Panamericana, pudo trabajar de todo corazón como Americanista, en la plena convicción que los problemas del Hemisferio: de libertad, de derechos humanos, de cooperación intelectual, son problemas fundamentales del siglo y del mundo.

Para concluir, la Dra. Lee aludió a una de las declaraciones del propio Juan Marín, al ser interrogado qué concepto suyo le gustaría que fuera considerado como su

contribución ideológica a la Unión Panamericana, y Juan
Marín respondió: "Desearía que, a pesar de que los años
pasen, quede siempre indeleble la noción por la que siempre
he luchado, para que sea verdad esa identificación absoluta
y estricta entre la cultura y el concepto de la libertad. . . ."

30. *Congressional Record*. Vol. 109, Friday, March 9, 1963. No. 36,
page 3529. (Also see note 19 above.)

31. This telegram is among the papers of Doña Milena L. de Marín.

32. These are: *The Juan Marin Graduate Scholarship in Engineering*
established in the Federico Santa María Technical University in Santiago
and *The Juan Marin Educational Center* in Guayaquil, Ecuador.

33. *Instituto de Investigaciones de la Literatura Chilena*. This Organization, attached to the University of Chile in Santiago and for many
years under the leadership of Dr. César Bunster, has helped many native
Chileans as well as many foreigners with their studies in the literature
of Chile.

Chapter II

1. Juan Marin, Nascimento, Santiago: 1938. (See chapter III.)

2. Juan Marin. Nascimento, Santiago: 1944. (See chapter III.)

3. *El jardín profanado*. Roberto Meza Fuentes, Talca, Chile: Imprenta Mejía, 1916.

4. *Revista Aliados*. (magazine) Año I, No. 8, septiembre de 1917,
pp. 25-26.

5. *Selva Lírica*. (magazine) Año I, No. 5, Santiago: Octubre, 1917,
p. 19.

6. Juan Marin. *Looping*, Nascimento, Santiago: 1929, 118 pages.

7. Juan Marin. *Aquarium*, Editorial Walton, Santiago: 1928, p. 23.

8. *Diario latino*. (newspaper) San Salvador, El Salvador: February 24,
1945. (First published in *Gong*, Valparaíso, 1930.)

9. "*Klaxon*." *Ariel* (magazine) No. 2, Santiago: 1925; "Buenos Aires."
Andarivel (magazine) No. 1, Santiago: May, 1927.

10. "Boxing." *La Nación* (newspaper) Santiago: August 27, 1924;
"Superavión." *La Nación* (newspaper) Santiago: October 15, 1924.

11. "Boxing," "Shimmy," and "Yankilandia." *PROA* (magazine) Buenos
Aires: Año II, March 1925, pp. 20-27.

12. In spite of the relative silence with which *Looping* was received
in 1929, it is well to note that a few outstanding critics recognized that
Juan Marin's first book of poems could not be so easily dismissed. The
following are only a few criticisms published soon after the appearance
of *Looping:* Gregorio Guerra. *Ultimas noticias*. May 13, 1929; Benjamín

Jarnes. *Revista de las Españas.* July, 1929; Serafín Ortega. *Los andes.*
Mendoza, Arg., January 3, 1930: Doctor Pangloss (Plinio Enríquez).
Boletín médico de Chile. June 15, 1929; Salvador Reyes. *Letras.* July,
1929; Arturo Trunkoso. *Austral.* October 1929; Alejandro Galaz. *Mundo
social.* December, 1932; Orestes Plath. (pseud.) *El trabajo.* August 10,
1932.

13. "Spin." *Looping.* pp. 5-13. We are indebted to Carlos and Esther
Vallejo for their excellent and inspired translations to English found in
this chapter. The parenthetical notes indicate the book and page of the
original publication. E.g. (p. 5-L) means that "Spin" is to be found on
page 5 of *Looping.*

14.   Canción . . . Oh . . . Canción   (p. 5-L)
        la de acero esta mañana
        partida en 100 tajadas rubias
        y envuelta en vendas de algodón.

15. LA VIDA   (p. 13-L)
        sadismo de azules
                dolor
haciendo una piltrafa de episodios
TIERRA
        abierta
                contra fuselajes rotos
                    sin ADIOS
y el ESPIRITU libre
        jugando al escondite
            con el sol . . .

16.   sobre el trampolín de los vientos vírgenes (p. 21-L)
        la mariposa férrea ha brincado
        un corazón piloto sale a caza
        de constelaciones
        anteojos tetraédricos chaquetas
        impermeables para el desconcierto
        rrrrrrrrrrrrrrrrrrrr . . .
        se ha perdido en las fuerzas múltiples   (p. 26-L)
        el corazón del hombre sigue
        sigue
        ascendiendo en los vórtices infinitos
        en el telón del universo
        se proyectan los signos
        gritos astrales
        nacen se rompen y mueren en sí mismos
        más allá de las líneas en la danza

de horizontes enanos y de siglos microscópicos
más allá de los astros sobre el polvo
de oro atómico de las constelaciones
sobre el galope de las ideologías
en medio de las sombras del Cósmos
el Hombre afirma su existencia milenearia
con el superavión de su pensamiento

17.   volando sobre 5000 metros   (p. 111-L)
he querido hacer esta mañana un looping
me acompañaba "Saxofón"
un negro pekinés que es mi mascota
y mi única preocupación

. . . . .

18.   estamos en 3000 oh! cuánto falta   (p. 117-L)
          para entrar en el reino de Dios

. . . . .

19.   pero ya es tiempo de bajar   (p. 118-L)
          "piquemos"
y digamos adiós
                abajo
todo igual estará siempre
la casa
      los tranvías
             Marión

20.   Cámaras fotográficas baldes esponjas   (p. 14-L)
hombres de jockey y camiseta blanca
caras de apaches ultracivilizados
oficiando en cenáculos de magia
en los ángulos rectos del ringside

. . . . .

21.   brazos que terminan en tumores negros   (p. 15-L)
línea de carnes en el aire
danza de biceps y de pantorrillas
¡en guarda . . . up! . . . uppercut!!!

22.   música que   (p. 105-L)
tiene el ritmo extraño de las cosas mecánicas
el compás de las olas bajo los hidroaviones
a compás de los sístoles y los diástoles
electro-cardíaco-dinámicos
de los corazones

. . . . .

23.   Fot-Trot   (p. 106-L)

divino baile de los Mr. y de las Miss   (pp. 106-7-L)
en un gigante avance
de Atila o de Nemrod
pasaste de Washington a París
te bailamos como los monigotes articulados
el alma toda tuya es un resorte muscular
piernas y brazos enlazados
y entremezclados
como las aguas
en el mar
cuando entras hipando en los salones
se siente un hálito a bencina
y un sonar de cristales
en los mesones
de una cantina
guiñapos de bandas de guarnición
danzan en la orquestación
la música de líjas está loca
un negro con resortes en la boca
quiebra su propio record
en trombón!!

24.   Atlantic cabaret   *(Not published in either LOOPING*
de Colón: *or AQUARIUM.)*
Marineros acrobáticos danzando
O.K. . . . . O.K. . . .
El Saxofón
el fox, la conga y rumba y el black bottom
y el danzón . . .

. . . .
Las caras muestran dientes blancos
y sudor.
Es todo el ritmo y es la "syncopation"
de hoy.

. . . .
¡Cantan los dólares sobre los cristales
con un lírico canto de motor!
Mujeres de Hawaii,
mujeres de Luzón,
piernas de Broadway y de Filipinas
de Sidney y de Saigón.

. . . .

Merceditas, muchacha de Jamaica,
bebamos nuestro sherry taciturno
y bailemos el fox,
y después, cuando el alba inunde el cielo,
digamos adiós.

. . . .

¡Merceditas, negrita de Jamaica,
hija del Africa, nacida
en tierras de Cristóbal Colón . . . !
¡Pequeña taxi-girl sin patria, sin
pasado y sin Dios . . . !

25. Andrés Sabella. *El Mercurio de Santiago.* Feb. 8, 1946.

Of all the criticisms of Juan Marin's poetry that we have read, the one we cite here written by Andrés Sabella is the most judicious, the most scholarly, and the most penetrating. Sabella's article deserves to be quoted in full, but we shall have to content ourselves with a few lines:

Poeta, hermano de Apollinaire, Juan Marín resplandece
en todas las proas que avanzan, acariciando el rostro de un
mañana venturoso para el mundo: el mensaje de su *Looping* viaja hoy día, jubilosamente en la triunfante realidad
de los espacios domados por el hombre.

26. Orestes Plath in *Alas sobre el mar,* Editorial Documentos, pp. 239-240 Santiago:

Toda la obra realizada desde el año 1924 es como un
receptor de la emoción dinámica que se ajusta al ritmo de
la época y en que el siglo le entrega sus mejores jugos.

. . . . . .

En cuanto a la atracción por el deporte, se sitúan en
nuestra América: Fernán Silva Valdés domando potros a
lazo; Parra de Riego, recolector de polirritmo, cantando al
fútbol: . . . . Así en Marín´como en muchos de estos poetas
está 'el afán por las cosas y actividades mecánicas,
máquinas, muñecos, cinematógrafo, automovilismo, aviación; . . .'

27. Oh poema de acero que abraza el mundo nuevo (p. 16 Aq.)
grito de bronquios de la usina
tus rimas son los ejes biselados
fulgurantes de voluntad dinámica

. . . . . .

mecánica canción sistema
filosofía oculta de una incógnita alquimia
ha de surgir el HOMBRE

que te muestre desnuda
que viole tus secretos
vuelque tu corazón en tus retortas
los queme en tus hornazas
y escriba
la nueva lírica
la de las líneas rectas
la de los fuselajes
la de las altas antenas
y de las ruedas infinitamente veloces
que te empujan

. . . .

28. El cielo se ha ido tan arriba   (pp. 10-11 Aq.)
porque arrojó el lastre de las nubes
de su barquilla azul
nos miran los jemelos telescópicos
de dos farolas vespertinas
observatorio
de la colina sin nombre
salud
buena muchacha
mientras las barcas vienen
a amarrarse a sus muelles
ves
la NOCHE
    está encendiendo
             sus fuegos
en sus negras calderas
    ya crepitan las chispas allá arriba
Y PONE PROA AL ALBA.

29. Un esqueleto danza en la nieve   (p. 12-Aq.)
    blanco como un sueño
        y la luna lo envuelve
        y le azulea los huesos . . .
            Un esqueleto danza en la nieve.

30. En el crepúsculo de fuego   (p. 13 Aq.)
    la mariposa vuela
        su diminuto y rojo velo
        acaricia como una lengua . . . .
        En el crepúsculo de fuego.

31. Canta de pájaro en el alba   (p. 13 Aq.)
    melodiosa candileja

música con que ametrallan
el alma de la arboleda . . . .
Canto de pájaro en el alba.

32. Onda glauca que va y viene   (p. 15 Aq.)
y acaricia y amenaza
alarga un muslo de nieve
y se aleja hacia las albas . . . .
Onda glauca que va y viene.

33. Another popular poet and accredited lecturer on poetics, Vicente
Huidobro (1893-1948), is considered the theorist of *creationism*. (See
pp. 263-265 of *Literatura hispanoamericana*. Anderson Imbert, Enrique
y Eugenio Florit, Edición revisada, 1970, Vol. II, for a summary and
discussion of Huidobro's concept of *creationism*.) Huidobro influenced
greatly the group of poets who were becoming known during the third
and fourth decades of the Twentieth Century. We may well imagine that
such poems as "Mancha cromática," "Nocturno," and "Paisaje" published
in *Aquarium* show the influence of Huidobro. En *Atenea,* Año XLV, Tomo
CLXVII, no. 420, pp. 169-252 were published two fundamental studies
of Huidobro: "Vicente Huidobro y el creacionismo" by Braulio Arenas
and "La práctica huidobriana" by Ana Pizarro, both very important for
an understanding of *creationism*. The second study includes many of
Huidobro's best poems. It is our belief, however, that poems such as
"Atlantic cabaret" that have a story, that avoid extremes of *creationism,*
are Marin's best.

34. In some of the following chapters, e.g. "Philosophies . . ." and
"Travel and Interpretation" we have quoted generously from some of
Juan Marin's translations from English and French poetry to Spanish. We
cannot, however, refrain from giving a sample here:

El Egipto de los faraones. p. 291:

Tengo hoy la muerte frente a mí
como el fluir del arroyuelo lento
como el regreso del marino al puerto.

Like all Chileans, Dr. Marin was justly proud of the poetry of Gabriela
Mistral, Chile's contribution to the list of Nobel Prize winners; he com-
pares "Tengo la muerte frente a mí" to one of the well-loved poems of
La divina Gabriela:

Este largo cansancio se hará mayor un día
y el alma dirá al cuerpo que no quiere seguir
arrastrando su peso por la rosada vía
por donde van los hombres contentos de vivir.

(And this great weariness will become greater

And the soul will say to the body that it does not wish
To continue dragging itself along the rosy path where are
found the men who are still content to live.)

Chapter III

1. See *Bibliographies*.
2. *La Nación*. Santiago, Chile: October 7, 1934.
3. Editorial Julio Walton, Santiago: 1934, 242 pages.
4. *Margarita, el aviador y el médico*. Zig-Zag, Santiago: 1952, 96 pages.
5. Salvador Reyes in "Prólogo" to *Alas sobre el mar*. p. 7:
   Alas sobre el mar es un bello libro, escrito por un soñador enamorado del misterio y el peligro . . . *Alas* . . . posee la primera virtud de todo buen libro; invita a leer, atrae, interesa. . . .
6. See also "Puerto las ánimas" in *Cuentos de viento y agua*, p. 110 ff.
7. Roberto Brenes Mesén. *Lázaro de Betanía*. (Ediciones Convivio), San José, Costa Rica: 1932.
8. "Lázaro" and "El techo . . ." were included in *El secreto . . .*, Ercilla, (*Colección contemporáneos*), Santiago: 1936, pp. 145-168.
9. "Viaje en el 'Hurricane'" (Voyage on the "Hurricane"). *El Mercurio*, 22 de mayo de 1964. (Posthumous publication.)
10. "Hielos magallánicos en un campo de concentración de Shanghai." (We have seen only a reprint of this item in a special edition of *Diario latino*, San Salvador, El Salvador: Feb. 24, 1945.)
11. *Atenea*. "El derrumbe del cielo." No. 322, pp. 60-78.
12. Nicomedes Guzmán. *Antología de cuentos chilenos*. Nascimento, Santiago: 1965, 503 pages. (A more appropriate title for this story would have been "Death of el Chilote Grande.")
13. Roberto Sarah C. *Atenea*. No. 321, pp. 331-333. "Juan Marín, aventurero: sus 'Cuentos de viento y agua.'"
   Este hombre alto y definido, este poeta y psicoanalista, traductor, viajero inquieto y trota mundos. . . . No se olvida de su suelo ni de sus hombres ni de lo que aquí amó, soñó, planeó e hizo. Fue Chile su trampolín para la distancia, para infinita distancia que él ha cubierto sin vanagloria, pero con sed de aventura; . . . de la *realidad y la fantasía*. (Our italics.)
   Pocas veces habíamos advertido mejor amalgamados ambos ingredientes, el del ensueño y el del realismo, que en las obras de Juan Marín. . . .
   No sabemos, . . . qué nos atrae más en estos catorce

fuertes relatos: si el extraordinario humanismo . . . o la
desatada violencia de una imaginación que no tiene
tregua. . . .

14. *Margarita.* . . . p. 95.

> Su carrero era una fuga sin término . . .
> era una huida infinita y eterna . . .
> era una huida de sí misma . . .

15. Hernán Diaz Arrieta (Alone). *La Nación.* Julio 31 de 1932.

Un crítico, en buenas cuentas, no debería hablar mal
sino de los libros que no ha leído, mejor dicho, que no ha
podido leer por culpa del aburrimiento o cualquier otra
culpa análoga. Si llega a la última página sin saltarse
punto ni coma, está perdido; quiera que no quiera, debe
elogiar. Nadie sino los héroes o los cándidos se sienten
obligados a echarse al cuerpo todo un volumen desagradable
para decir luego que les ha desagradado. Claro que los
autores opinan de distinta manera; ellos encuentran ilícito
juzgar del contenido de sus toneles por unos cuantos
tragos de vino; mas para que los autores y críticos se
pongan de acuerdo habrá que esperar la nueva . . .

He aquí que hemos leído íntegra la novela del Dr. Juan
Marín, titulada *Margarita, el aviador y el médico,* que edita
la Biblioteca Zig-zag y prologa Hernán del Solar.

16. Luis Durand. *El Mercurio.* Septiembre 6 de 1932.

Al autor de este libro, personalmente, casi no lo conozco.
Unas dos veces apenas, hemos conversado breves palabras
con él. Por lo demás esto no tiene importancia, para poder
formarse un juicio acerca de su obra intelectual, bien
nutrida y tesonera. Hacemos esta referencia, únicamente
porque nos ha llamado la atención, la actividad asombrosa
que despliega este joven de anchos hombros y recias man-
díbulas, más a propósito para recibir los golpes de un
boxeador, que el cosquilleo de las pullas y agudezas, a
veces un poco fuera de tono, de nuestros críticos oficiales.
Y, sin saber cómo, hemos experimentado una espontánea
simpatía por este hombre que emplea tan noblemente su
juventud y su talento. En un día, recordamos haber leído
su crónica de libros, luego le vimos interviniendo en un
debate de la *Sociedad de Escritores,* a donde seguramente
llegaba después de ver a algún enfermo en su consultorio,
o de asistir a una operación en el hospital. Y en la noche,
de ese mismo día, mientras comíamos en un restorán

del centro, le oímos por la radio, dando una conferencia sobre temas de su profesión . . .

Y este dinamismo personal, Juan Marín sabe comunicárselo a sus personajes y a los acontecimientos, ocurridos en el curso de sus relatos.

"En suma, *Margarita* . . . es un libro lleno de simpatía que como un amigo cordial, nos cuenta la fibra orgánica en un relato, para que éste resulte interesante."

17. Ernesto Montenegro. "Prólogo" to *Un avión volaba (A Plane Was Flying)*. Ediciones Ercilla. Santiago: 1955, p. 9.

En la presente novela nos da algo como un epítome animado de sus múltiples vocaciones. Nos habla de la aviación en poeta, y nos presenta el aeroplano como el instrumento simbólico gracias al cual el hombre puede librarse de muchas miserias terrestres, ensanchar su visión del mundo y sentirse vivir con todas sus potencias bajo el estímulo arrebatador de la velocidad. En el aviador resume la humanidad del mañana.

18. Our novelist became interested in mental illnesses and conditions during his medical school days, but we feel justified in saying that he gave more and more attention to them as he accumulated experiences.

19. Ernesto Montenegro *Loc. cit.*

En cuanto a sus aciertos de novelista, diré solamente que desde las primeras lineas de esta novela se encuentra planteado el conflicto en la oposición de los caracteres y en el vigor de los incidentes dramáticos. La atención del lector despierta desde el primer momento como un arco tenso al que no ha de soltar ya la mano que lo empuña.

20. Ernesto Rodríguez Mendoza. "Prólogo" a *Paralelo 53 sur.* (Primera edición), Nascimento, 1936. pp. 7 and 9.

Me dijeron que era (Juan Marín) un hombre grandote, con la gorra de marino echada al ojo y enamorado de las hélices y los volantes . . . Andaba buscando su camino literario.

No siempre ha sido fácil que un escritor lo encuentre desde el primer momento. . . .

Pensé pedirle formalmente que dejara el avión sobre las nieves magallánicas y se pusiera de una vez en marcha hacia la realidad, porque es evidente que el que dispone de una imaginación a hélice verá la vida, dondequiera que la enfoque, con un relieve que nunca lograrán dar los simples peatones.

21. Juan Marín. "Sinopsis," *Paralelo* . . . p. 38.

No quisiéramos repetir lo que esos labios (i.e. lips of Magellan) cuatrocentenarios dicen, pero invitamos al lector a adivinar, leyendo estas páginas de dolor, de injusticia y de muerte.

22. Luis Merino Reyes. "Juan Marín, médico, cuentista, novelista." *Interamerican Review of Bibliography*, OAS. Washington, D. C.: Jan. - Mar., 1964, pp. 3-20. (With an excellent bibliography prepared by Frank P. Hebblethwaite.)

Paralelo 53 sur, novela publicada por primera vez en 1936 por la Editorial Nascimento, merecedora del *Premio Municipal de Literatura* de ese año, prologada por Emilio Rodríguez Mendoza, Francisco Ferrándiz Alborz y Elías Castelnuovo: traducida en trozos al inglés por Harriet de Onís y al portugués por la Editorial "Renascenca" de Lisboa, ha sido considerada la mejor producción de Juan Marín. Es, al menos, su novela más popular, aquélla que le justifica como vigoroso escritor, aun para los más incrédulos de su valía, nunca escasos en Chile, si de enjuiciar se trata. . . .

23. *Naufragio*. p. 83.

¡Allá! ¡Allí! -me gritó—. ¡Mira, un barco con rumbo a nosotros! ¡Estamos salvados! ¡Es el capitán—nuestro capitán querido—que viene a buscarnos!

24. *Op. cit.* p. 10.

Por eso, dedico a él — y a todos los hombres de mar de mi país que constantemente se juegan la vida en los mares australes — este relato mitad real, mitad fantástico, como la vida misma.

25. We were surprised to find so few references to Constitución and Talca in Dr. Marín's writings. On reading *Orestes* . . ., however, we were struck with an irresistible desire to see Talca, where he spent four years in the liceo (secondary school), to make the round-trip on the *trencito de trocha angosta* (narrow gauge train), and to see for ourselves the Maule River as it empties into the Pacific at Constitución. Our some four hours, time between the arrival of the train from the north to its departure for Talca, gave us, we feel, a better appreciation of *Orestes* . . . and of the novelist. In spite of his warning that the reader must not accept as autobiographical what the writer lets filter through his

imaginative inventions, there is always something gained by a personal exploration of the scenes described. (See *Orestes* . . . pp. 38-58.)

26. *Conventillo.* The famous dictionary, *Pequeño Larousse Ilustrado,* defines *conventillo,* "Casa de vecindad donde vive mucha gente pobre." The *conventillo* is peculiar to Argentina and Chile. It is perhaps in the writings of José Santos González Vera that one gets the clearest idea of how squalid life can be in the *conventillo,* especially as presented in *Cuando era muchacho, Vidas mínimas,* and *Alhué.*

27. (See *Advertencia* in the Nascimento edition of *Viento* . . . , 1944.)
Así como *Paralelo* . . . aspiró a captar un aspecto de nuestra patria incógnita, *Viento* . . . intenta aprisionar otro. Más tarde—si el destino así lo permite—verá la luz *Desierto fecundo,* con el cual se cerrará la Triología que nos propusimos.

28. Mario Bahamonde. *Antología del cuento nortino.* University of Chile, 1966, 369 pages.
Mario Bahamonde has worked diligently to encourage writings about the north of Chile. For years, also, Andrés Sabella has at great personal sacrifice inspired and encouraged many promising writers to produce novels and stories about the northern provinces. Juan Marín's projected novel, *Desierto fecundo,* would, we believe, have contributed much to the literature of north Chile.

29. *Viento negro.* Zig-zag edition 1960, Santiago: (See inside cover) "Sin embargo, lo más valioso de la obra de Juan Marín se halla contenido, sin duda, en sus novelas, entre las cuales basta citar *La muerte de Julián Aranda, Un avión volaba, Paralelo 53 sur, Muerte en Shanghai.* . . ."

30. Luis Merino Reyes. *Op. cit.* p. 6.
Y ya que hemos nombrado a otros autores, diremos que Juan Marín había leído muy bien a Joseph Conrad, a Blaise Cendrars, a quien tradujo; a Somerset Maughan, de quien acaso aprendió a ser ameno, por encima de todo y, también, como lo hemos visto, al Guillaume Apollinaire prosista, . . . Sólo que la imaginación de Marín se mantenía fiel a una inquietud metafísica, . . . lo que es más paradójico dado su hábito profesional de médico, a tono con las religiones y cofradías iniciáticas que su curiosidad infatigable lo llevó a frecuentar. . . .

31. *Loc. Cit.*
Perdía rápidamente la noción de lo real y entraba en el encantado mundo de los sueños.

32. *Op. cit.* p. 8.

Alguna vez oímos a cierto escritor fenomenal chileno, que hablaba de sí mismo, acerca de la importancia de la literatura imaginista, única o muy escasa dentro del realismo geográfico, ubicable por zonas marinas, campesinas y urbanas de la literatura chilena. Pensamos entonces como ahora que, en esa latitud literaria, Juan Marín ha sido incomprendido y, por ello mismo, olvidado. La mayoría de sus cuentos y la resolución de sus novelas, *Viento negro*, por ejemplo, tienen un acento imaginativo, el salto de la realidad monótona y opresora, que acaso le viene al autor de su carácter andariego, con un sentido muy claro de que la literatura es artificioso fabulador, hecho verosímil dentro de sus límites propios, pero extraordinario. Tal fuerza imaginativa está armonizada tanto en lo que los personajes dicen como en lo que hacen.

33. Luis Merino Reyes. *Op. cit.* p. 16.

Y así continuamos seducidos, sin poder rematar estas líneas, por los tesoros artísticos de Juan Marín. . . . Juan Marín pertenece a esos valores humanos que saben o guardan apasionadamente la concordancia entre sus medios y sus fines. La finalidad del doctor Juan Marín fue escribir novelas, cuentos, ensayos, divulgar culturas, defender con ella la libertad del pensamiento, la decencia, la dignidad del hombre. Sus medios fueron la lejanía de su patria, extendida en la última baranda del mundo, que acaso no le dio lo que él mereció, y su cuerpo que un día— testigo y resistencia de muchas andanzas—no lo quiso seguir. Pero estos hombres superiores que han pasado a nuestro lado, que han vivido al alcance de nuestros dedos, nos hacen creer un poco en la quimera de la gloria y en la inmortalidad.

34. Enrique Anderson Imbert. *Literatura hispanoamericana.* Tomo II, pp. 225-6. Fondo de cultura económica, México-Buenos Aires: 2 vols. 1961.

Algunos narradores se escapan de la realidad por el lado del mar, de la ventura, del ensueño, de la fantasía seudocientífica . . .

Aunque Juan Marín es autor, entre muchos otros libros, de una descripción de la vida sufrida en el *Paralelo 53 sur,* tiene también una dimensión fantástica, como se ve en sus *Cuentos de viento y agua.*

35. José A. Balseiro. *Expresión de hispanoamérica—Segunda parte.*

Instituto de Cultura Puertorriqueña. San Juan, P. R.: 1963, pp. 155-76. (See also *Paralelo 53 sur, Mercurio* 19 de diciembre de 1965.)

El número de los cuadros de perversidad, sin resquicio por donde asome el optimismo, y las sombras que invariablemente anegan con sus olas malditas a las almas que aquí transitan, no nos parecen nunca fabricación convencional o mecánica del novelista. Todo se desarrolla con legítimo aliento de veracidad. . . . Este (Juan Marín) supo pintar antes y con maestría cuadros de inolvidable y consistente valor, no sujetos ni a las circunstancias políticas ni a los arbitrajes de derecho.

. . . . .

En una y otra obras (*Paralelo* . . . and *Viento* . . .) verificamos el genuino interés del autor en los problemas sociales del proletariado y de los humildes. Los hechos transcurren en *Viento* . . . tan plásticamente representados que los seguimos como si fuéramos testigos oculares.

Aunque los personajes y sus dichos son inconfundiblemente chilenos, su sentimiento es universal. Así lo evidencia la melancolía que nos deja su conflicto la verdad, sugerida en la buena fe de Pedro, al ser derrotado por la malévola estupidez de sus delatores: conflicto que conduce a la catástrofe y la muerte de todo un pueblo.

La estimación de Juan Marín por la Marina de Guerra de su república, es patente. Más de una vez le hace justicia. Su amor al mar, aparece y reaparece con lírica exaltación. Y la angustia económica—donde la baja de la moneda y el alza del costo de existir simbolizan todo un drama personal y nacional—hace de *Viento* . . . inolvidable documento de la vida difícil, y tantas veces patética, en aquella tierra.

36. *Op. cit.* p. 165.

. . . Todo se desarrolla con legítimo aliento de veracidad. Sin embargo, habría, a nuestro juicio, que exceptuar el capítulo último. En éste nos parece que el chileno en Juan Marín le llevó la mano al escritor.

37. *Orestes y yo (Orestes and I)*. Ediciones "Asia-América." Tokio, Japón: 1940. *El emperador Kwang Hsü (The Emperor Kwang Hsü)*. Ediciones "Asia-América." Tokio, Japón: 1941.

38. Juan Marin. *Orestes and I*. Ediciones "Asia-América." Tokio, Japón: 1940. (Translated by Richard P. Butrick.)

39. *Orestes y yo* p. 64.

40. Juan Marin. *El emperador Kwang Hsü (The Emperor Kwang Hsü)*. Ediciones "Asia-América." Tokio, Japón: 1941. (Translated by Richard P. Butrick.)

41. *El emperador Kwang Hsü.* p. 136.

> ¡La Dinastía ha muerto . . . . Pero China sólo ha
> estado dormida! ¡China vivirá!!! ¡China es eterna!!!

Chapter IV

1. This very important chapter deserves a book-length study; we sincerely hope that some student, whose orientation and preparation include more than a superficial acquaintance with the philosophies and religions of the Far East, will accept the challenge to study this material more thoroughly.

2. Juan Marin. *El Tibet misterioso y sus lamas (Mysterious Tibet and Her Lamas)*. Nascimento, Santiago: 1944, 172 pages.

3. *El Tibet* . . . . pp. 139-142: (Juan Marin introduces the poem.)
   > Como ejemplo característico de literatura religiosa lamaísta,
   > hemos querido traducir el canto "Nirvana," del poeta
   > místico tibetano Milarespa, del cual acabamos de hablar en
   > el capítulo anterior.

4. We include a generous quotation from Dr. Marin's translation to Spanish of this poem "Nirvana":
   > Rétchungpá que te asemejas a mi corazón,
   > escucha este canto de preceptos que encierra mi última voluntad:
   > En el océano de la transmigración de los Tres Mundos
   > El cuerpo irreal es el gran pecador.
   > Mientras nos preocupemos del alimento y los vestidos
   > no hay verdadero renunciamiento al mundo.
   > ¡Oh! ¡Renuncie al mundo, Rétchungpá!
   > En la ciudad de los cuerpos irreales
   > el alma irreal es la gran pecadora.
   > Sometida a la carne y a la sangre del cuerpo,
   > ella no tiene jamás noción de su propia naturaleza.
   > ¡Oh! ¡Discierne la naturaleza del alma, Rétchungpá!
   > En los confines del espíritu y la materia
   > el conocimiento, creado por sí mismo, es el gran culpable
   >
   > . . . . . .
   >
   > En la ciudad turbadora de las seis Clases de Seres
   > la ceguera del pecado es inmensa.
   > El espíritu sigue los impulsos del amor y del odio
   > y no percibe la igual inexistencia de las cosas.

¡Oh! ¡Rechaza amor y odio, Rétchungpá!
En el seno del espacio inmaterial
El Buda Perfecto suscita imágenes equívocas.
El ha mostrado la seducción del mundo aparente:

. . . . .

Adora en conjunto, como Trinidad Unidad,
Lamas, "Ydams" y Dioses,
reunidas en un Todo;
Contemplación, Meditación y Extasis.
Acostúmbrate a no considerar sino como Una cosa
a esta vida, la próxima y los limbos.

. . . . .

¡Esta es mi última enseñanza!
Este es el fin de mi testamento:
después, ¡nada más existe, oh Rétchungpá!(5)

5. (Note by Juan Marin.)
   Nótese cuán pura se encuentra la Doctrina de Buda en
esta composición a pesar de haber sido compuesta por un
místico heterodoxo tibetano. El más ortodoxo "hinayanista"
no la hubiera expresado de manera más perfecta.

6. Juan Marin. *Lao-Tszé o el universalismo mágico (Lao-Tszé or the
Magical Universe)*. Espasa-Calpe, Buenos Aires: *(Colección austral)* 1952.
(First published as lead essay in Dr. Marin's longer book, *China: Lao-
Tszé, Confucio, Buda*. Espasa-Calpe, Buenos Aires: 1944, 454 pages.)

7. Juan Marin. *Confucio o el humanismo didactizante (Confucius
or Didactic Humanism)*. Espasa-Calpe, Buenos Aires: 1954, (Segunda
edición) 147 pages. (This was first published in the book *China*. See
note 6 above.)

8. *Confucio . . .* p. 141 ff.

EL TEMPLO DE CONFUCIO EN PEKING

A la sombra de viejos y robustos cipreses que fueron
plantados por los emperadores mongoles en pleno siglo
XII de nuestra era, alza hoy—en un quieto rincón de la
hormigueante "ciudad tártar"—sus muros rojos y sus
techos amarillos, el "Kung Miao" o templo de Kung.

Una gran sencillez caracteriza su arquitectura: es un
edificio sin lirismos ni audacias, grave y adusto, de líneas
simples y pesadas, tal cual hubiera placido al maestro. No
hay tampoco ídolos en su interior ni esculturas ni brocados

en sus paredes y altares. No debiera llamarse templo, sino palacio o tal vez hogar o recinto.

. . . . .

En el patio principal, lo primero que llama la atención son los célebres "tambores de piedra," macizos cilindros de granito negro, con sus caras totalmente revestidas de inscripciones en que está grabada la más antigua historia de China. . . .

Al fondo de este patio arbolado y fragante de aromas vegetales, bajo cuyas avenidas repasaban sus lecciones los candidatos a los famosos "Exámenes Imperiales" del pasado, se yergue la silueta imponente de la "Cámara de la Gran Perfección." Es este pabellón, una de las joyas más preciadas del Peking arquitectónico y artístico, sus columnas y puertas labradas están hechas con la más fina madera de teca, traída de Birmania e Indochina. El interior es sobrio: en el centro, sobre una especie de esotérico trono, puede verse la "tableta" del maestro, con esta sencilla inscripción: "Tableta del alma del antecesor y filósofo más sagrada: Confucio."

9. *Op. cit.* p. 145.

En su conjunto, la enseñanza de Confucio es un formidable sistema de ética constreñido por el rito y enaltecido por un noble—aunque mesurado—impulso de fraternidad —¡no igualdad!—universal.

No busquemos en él éxtasis místicos ni tampoco concesiones al demonio. Es sólo un cuerpo de doctrinas positivas, tendientes a mejorar el estado de cosas en la tierra, sin preocuparse poco ni mucho del Más Allá, como no sea reverenciar a los antepasados.

10. Juan Marin. *Buda o la negación del mundo (Buddha or the Rejection of the World).* Espasa Calpe, Buenos Aires: 1954, 226 pages. (This also was first published as part of *China. . . .* See note 6, above.)

11. *Buda. . . .* p. 224.

Tomado en su esencia y con todas las variantes que él ha sufrido en veinticinco siglos, es el de Buda un mensaje moral cargado de intensos elementos poéticos y emocionales. Su recado se alzó desde los planos del dolor y la miseria hacia los cielos de la Etica para descender de nuevo entre los hombres.

El budismo creó 'complejos' ético-estéticos de belleza no igualada. La serenidad del rostro juvenil del dios, la

armonía de su cuerpo en reposo, son ecuaciones de la más
depurada belleza teoantropomórfica.

12. *Op. cit.* p. 225.

El budismo no fue en China religión de letrados y de
mandarines, como el confucianismo ni derivó hacia el
laboratorio heirofántico del astrólogo-alquimista, como el
taoísmo. Fue, desde el momento mismo en que entró en
contacto con el pueblo chino, una religión de los humildes
y un consuelo para los desamparados.

13. Juan Marin. *El alma de China (The Soul of China)*. Editorial
Claridad, Buenos Aires. *Biblioteca la tierra y el hombre.* Vol. 6, 1945,
442 pages.

14. *La India eterna (Eternal India)* p. 109. (This publication will be
discussed in the following chapter "Travel and Interpretation.")

. . . No podemos dejar de recordar en estos instantes
los ya lejanos años en que, rodeados de soldados japoneses
por todos lados, trabajamos en China, asiduamente y con
pasión, como para olvidar toda la sangre y el horror que
había en torno a nosotros, en nuestro estudio sobre el
budismo chino, que habría de integrar después nuestra
obra *China.*

15. *El alma . . .* p. 77.

NOSTALGIA

Frente a mi lecho
el resplandor de la Luna extiende
su escarcha de cristal sobre la Tierra
Alzo los ojos para contemplar el astro brillante.
Pienso en mi aldea
y entonces, mi cabeza se inclina.

16. *Chinese Jade.* Editorial Al-Hilal. Cairo, Egypt: 1948, p. 29.

17. *El alma . . .* pp. 190-191.

18. Juan Marin. *Mesa de mah-jong (The Mah-jong Table).* Buenos
Aires: Editorial Emecé, 1948, 363 pages.

19. *Mesa . . .* pp. 7-9.

PROLOGO

Caminar por las calles de una ciudad china significa
desafiar una avalancha de impresiones sensoriales múltiples; desde luego importa afrontar todos los olores, todas
las visiones, todos los contactos y todos los ruidos ima-
ginables. En China la calle es multitudinaria; en ella se

vive, algunas veces también en ella se muere, y puede aún darse el caso de que en ella se nazca. . . . Pues bien los mil y un sonidos que nos abruman cuando salimos a dar un paseo. . . . hay uno (ruido) muy peculiar que quien haya visitado el Florido Reino Medio no podrá olvidar jamás: ese ruido es una especie de tableteo de ametralladora que sale al través de una ventana abierta o escapa de una puerta semientornada. Se le escucha con más frecuencia en los barrios en que hay cocinerías, restaurantes y casas de té, pero no es exclusivo de ellos: se puede oír también en cualquier otro sector de la ciudad. Es un tictac que se adivina originado por un pequeño cuerpo duro al ser golpeado sobre una cubierta de madera. . . .

Se trata de un pasatiempo, del más inofensivo de los pasatiempos: el mah-jong de los chinos.

Mah-jong, teatro y té constituyen los paraísos terrenales de los amables y sufridos hijos de Han.

Generalmente, el mah-jong se juega de noche o al atardecer, cuando las faenas del día han terminado, pero también hay gentes que se pasan jugando el día entero. . . . Los hombres habitualmente juegan de noche. En una pieza atestada de gente y de objetos, bajo una luz central, hay una mesa cuadrada de madera muy sólida; en torno a la mesa cuatro sillas chinas, es decir, cuatro taburetas de madera sin respaldo ni cojines, y sentados en ellos cuatro jugadores. Alrededor puede haber o no muchos mirones; casi siempre los hay. Sobre las mesas las manos de los jugadores van arrojando los dominós de marfil con fuerza y rapidez increíbles. Jugado por los chinos, este juego no tiene pausas, vacilaciones ni demoras. Las jugadas van sucediéndose con un ritmo de hélice de avión.

. . . . .

Mesa de mah-jong hemos llamado a este libro. El no es más que un fichero de apuntes, notas e impresiones del País del Dragón. Sin reposo ni tardanza han sido escritos estos artículos al correr de los trenes, aviones y navíos, y con velocidad de proyectiles han sido lanzados después a los cuatro puntos cardinales del mundo.

20. *Op. cit.* pp. 50-51.

¡Hagamos una edición del 'Chin Ping Mei' y no nos faltará contante y sonante en las manos! —dice un personaje al otro en una crónica del siglo XVII.

Y así ha sido en efecto.

Traducida hace unos meses al inglés por Arthur Waley, la obra ha tenido enorme circulación. Viejos residentes europeos y americanos hemos encontrado en Peking que nos aseguran que la mejor manera de conocer y entender el alma china es leyendo el 'Chin Ping Mei'. En esta afirmación hay sin duda algunos elementos de verdad, pero en conjunto es una exageración. Nosotros creemos que la obra refleja fielmente una época de decadencia y corrupción de la sociedad, como todas las razas y naciones las han tenido. . . .

21. *Op. cit.* p. 89.

¡Oh! ¡Cómo es triste ser mujer!
No hay nada sobre la tierra que sea menos estimado;
los muchachos juegan junto a la puerta
como jóvenes dioses del Cielo.
Sus corazones están listos para desafiar los "Cuatro Océanos."

Chapter V

1. *El Egipto de los faraones (Egypt of the Pharaohs).* Zig-Zag, Santiago, Chile: 1954, 378 pages. *Colección historia y documentos.* Illustrated. (Tercera edición.)

2. *El Egipto* . . . p.12.

Este es, pues, un libro que intenta tratar principalmente sobre el Egipto de los faraones. Ocasionalmente inciden en él temas más modernos o colaterales. Esto no altera, sin embargo, el sentido fundamental de la obra, que es el de presentar una síntesis de impresiones y visiones recogidas por nosotros durante los años de nuestra residencia en el País del Nilo. De los cuatro planos o capas culturales que se superponen e imbican a lo largo de la historia egipcia: faraónica, griega o griego-romana, copta (cristiana) e islámica, nosotros nos hemos interesado esencialmente en las tres primeras, sin que eso significa menosvalorizar la última, que ha dado y sigue dando a Egipto grandes tesoros de arte y poderosas reservas de fe y valor.

3. *Op. cit.* pp. 290-291. (English translation made by R. O. Faulkner, *Journal of Egyptian Archeology.* Vol. 42: pp. 29-30.) Dr. Marin's translation to Spanish follows:

. . . Tengo hoy la Muerte frente a mí
como la convalecencia ante un enfermo,

como entrar a un jardín después del lecho.

. . . . .

Tengo hoy la Muerte frente a mí
como perfume de lotos abiertos,
cual el vaso de agua que calma al sediento.
Tengo hoy la Muerte frente a mí
como el fluir del arroyuelo lento,
como el regreso del marino al puerto.

. . . . .

Tengo hoy la Muerte frente a mí
como el paisaje del nativo pueblo
para el hombre que estuvo prisionero
y que retorna a su nativo suelo.

4. *Op. cit.* pp. 304-305.

  —Yo soy Isis. Mientras que yo salía al atardecer cumpliendo las órdenes de Tot, los Siete Escorpiones que me sirven de escolta salieron conmigo: Tefén y Befén, simpre tras de mí; Mestet y Mestetet, por debajo de mí, y Petet, Tetet y Metet me abren el camino. Yo les recomendé encarecidamente: "No reconozcáis al Negro, no saludéis al Rojo, no distingáis a un hijo de familia de un miserable. Mantened vuestros rostros bajos, mirando la senda. . . . Una campesina, viéndome fatigada, me abrió sus puertas y me invitó a descansar en su casa. Mientras tanto Tefén, que había entrado en la casa de la Gran Dama, picó al hijo de ésta. El fuego que se produjo en la casa de la Dama no había agua en el Cielo ni en la Tierra para extinguirlo. Y no era el tiempo de las lluvias. Aquella que no me abrió sus puertas sufría fuertemente en su corazón, ansiosa sin saber si el hijo de sus entrañas viviría o no. Ella recorría la villa lamentándose, pero nadie venía en su ayuda. Y he aquí por qué mi corazón tuvo piedad de aquel niño inocente y la llamé.

5. *Op. cit.* p. 306. Here we can only presume that this translation from an English or French text was made by Dr. Marin:

Atrás el rebelde de vil carácter
a quien Ra detuvo en su avance;
combatiendo aún en el seno materno,
realizando el mal, transgrediendo el recto camino
buscando el combate, gustando el desorden,
rehusando respeto a aquel que era su mayor.
Creando el mal, excitando el malestar

por hostilidad al padre de sus padres,
despreciando las leyes, obrando como bandido,
listo para matar y para robar. . . .

6. *Op. cit.* p. 380:

Hemos visto un mundo que fue, o acaso mejor, una sucesión de mundos que fueron y ya no son. Pero las piedras hablan y en ellas los signos están escritos. La caravana llega al borde de la fuente, contempla, medita y luego pasa. Y así por los siglos de los siglos.

Y ahora, lector benévolo, debemos también nosotros separarnos. Una sola lección quizás digna de aprender, entre muchas otras de efímera significación, debemos guardar de este libro: y ella es que el hombre, desde el comienzo de su historia, siendo un ser mortal ha ambicionado vivir como un inmortal.

7. *La India eterna (Eternal India).* Juan Marin. Zig-Zag, Santiago, Chile: (Segunda edición) 1956, 474 pages. Illustrated.

8. *La India* . . . p. 15.

En dos ocasiones hemos llegado a la India: la primera, viniendo de Oriente y entrando por Calcuta, la "Puerta del Este"; la segunda yendo desde Occidente y entrando por Bombay, La "Puerta del Oeste."

En cuatro años de permanencia en el País del Ganges recorrimos su extenso territorio desde las faldas del Himalaya hasta el cabo Comorín, desde Assam a Cachemira, de Darjeeling a Trivandrum, de Madrás a Udaipur. Hemos visitado y fotografiado la mayor parte de sus monumentos y entrado devotamente en sus más célebres santuarios. Tuvimos la suerte de conocer de cerca a algunos de sus hombres más importantes en el campo de la filosofía, la política y de la religión. . . . Nos contamos entre los primeros extranjeros que entraron en el reino de Nepal, después del golpe de Estado que abrió el país al viento de la libertad y el progreso; y siguiendo la huella de Rama, pasamos de la costa de Coromandel a la isla de Rameswaram y de allí a Ceylán. El valle de Cachemira, con sus lagos, sus ríos y nevadas montañas, fue nuestro sitio predilecto de solaz y descanso cuando el calor extenuante hacía la vida imposible en Delhi.

9. *Op. cit.* p. 65.

El "Taj-Mahal" es una tumba. Sin embargo, cuando se le contempla detenidamente y no con ojos de turista, sino de hombre permeable a la emoción y la belleza, se comprende que su construcción fue dictada por un amor tan profundo y apasionado que llegó mucho más allá de la muerte. Es un monumento esencialmente romántico, como un verso de Alfredo de Musset, como una tela de Delacroix, o como un nocturno de Chopin. —Hay que mirarlo a la luz de la luna—nos dice el guía—y verán ustedes allá arriba, bajo las estrellas, flotar el alma de los dos amantes en torno a la cúpola de mármol.

Porque el "Taj" es el poema de amor levantado por el emperador Jehan en memoria de su esposa Muntaz Mahal, o sea, la "Dama del Taj."

10. Vicente Blasco Ibáñez. *Vuelta al mundo de un novelista*. Valencia, Spain: 1926.

11. *Op. cit.* p. 192.

Llevando en sus cabellos ornados de flores fragantes
el áureo disco de la Luna,
este dios danza en el bello Vadougour
y me brinda su gracia y su amor.

12. *Op. cit.* p. 227.

En el remoto sureste de la India, allá donde las aguas del Mar de Arabia se juntan con las del Mar de Bengala y donde la distancia que separa a la isla de Ceylán del continente es tan corta que Rana pudo cruzarla sobre un puente de piedras construido por el "Dios-Mono" Hanuman y sus tribus de simios en la legendaria época del "Ramayana," se encuentra la Isla Sacra de Rameswaram, consagrada al culto de "Nuestro Señor Sivalinga," o sea Siva, bajo la forma fálica del "lingan". . . .

13. *Op. cit.* p. 439.

Y cuando decimos escúelas filosóficas entendemos decir también religiones, pues en la India las religiones no son teología sino filosofía.

Chapter VI

1. The medical writings of Juan Marin, those assembled in book form, are: *La tiro-toxicosis y su tratamiento quirúgico,* his doctoral dissertation which we are not analyzing; *Clínicas y maestros en Inglaterra y Francia; Poliedro médico; El problema sexual y sus nuevas fórmulas sociales;* and *Ensayos freudianos.* Although *Ensayos freudianos* deals with some subjects other than medical, we feel that this is the chapter in which it ought to be discussed.

2. *La tiro-toxicosis* . . . is a very significant study prepared as part of the requirements for the M.D. degree in Chile at the time. Such a study is no longer required of candidates for the M.D. degree in Chile. *La tiro-toxicosis y su tratamiento quirúgico.* (Tesis de licenciatura) Santiago, Soc. Imp. i Lit Universo, 1921, 150 pages.

3. Juan Marin. *Clínicas y maestros en Inglaterra y Francia. Boletín médico de Chile,* Valparaíso: 1931, 133 pages.

4. *Op. cit.* p. 7.

He aquí unos apuntes de viaje que la pluma trazara hace algunos meses, presurosa y liviana, en un viaje por Europa.

Fué unas veces en el silencio momentáneo de una habitación de hotel. Otras, en medio del fragor estridente de los trenes en marcha. Algunas, también, en la quietud infinita de un camarote por cuya claraboya asomaba un pedazo de horizonte azul.

. . . . .

Es mi intención solamente la de ofrecer diseños de hombres e instituciones, trazados en el medio mismo en que actúan.

. . . . .

Que estos apuntes sirvan, por lo menos, para despertar ese interés por los viajes y lecturas, que a mi juicio son el pan espiritual más necesario al médico de nuestro tiempo.

5. *Op. cit.* p. 17.

Para mí, Edimburgo es una de las ciudades más hermosas del mundo. Tiene la belleza bárbara y nebulosa de una Roma edificada en los confines del Septentrión.

Rodeada de suaves colinas al igual que la Ciudad Eterna, la perspectiva de sus amplias avenidas se decora de imponentes castillos de piedra y de ruinas y jardines. Las agujas pétreas de sus Catedrales recortan su perfil en el cielo bajo y gris. Pequeñas y tortuosas callejuelas desembocan como a escondidas en las grandes vías; el caminante, que por ellas se adentrare, encontrará el mismo encanto de los barrios viejos en las históricas ciudades: la callejuela empedrada limitada de altos muros y torreones obscurecidos por el tiempo, gradas que suben y bajan, y cruceros con el bebedero musgoso y la cruz enmohecida en el centro.

La historia y la leyenda parecen alentar como un perfume sutil y penetrante en el ambiente de la nobilísima capital de Escocia.

Su Castillo gigantesco como un monstruo dormido en el misterio de un silencio de siglos está lleno de la evocación del gran Robert The Bruce y del rudo pasado de glorias, sacrificios y muerte.

. . . . .

Pero dejemos a un lado las remembranzas históricas que con tal fuerza cautivan el espíritu en la hermosa villa. Y hablemos de su Universidad.

6. *Op. cit.* pp. 53-67.

7. *Op. cit.* pp. 91-95.

8. *Op. cit.* p. 95.

No apaguemos la única luz consoladora que nos va quedando en el alma.

9. Juan Marin. *Poliedro médico. Boletín médico de Chile,* Valparaíso: 1933, 201 pages.

10. *Poliedro* . . . pp. 5-6.

Es por eso que hemos querido reunir estas diversas y heterogéneas facetas de nuestra vida médico-literaria en un volumen.

. . . . .

Los 33 años de nuestra existencia han transcurrido un tanto febril, ansiosa y desarticuladamente. Nuestra curiosidad nos ha hecho acercarnos a las más variadas fuentes de conocimientos y de sensibilidad.

11. *Op. cit.* p. 9.

Hace 12 años, sin haber alcanzado todavía el título universitario que permite ejercer la medicina en Chile, llegué a la clínica del profesor Lucas Sierra como concursante al alto honor de pertenecer al grupo de colaboradores del maestro de esa clínica.

He de inspirarme, pues, en su ejemplo y seguir las tradiciones suyas en la letra y en el espíritu.

. . . . .

Agradezco al Sr. Vicerrector de la Universidad, don Pedro Godoy, al Sr. Decano don Armando Larraguibel, y a mi respetado amigo el Dr. Luis Bisquert . . . la participación que ellos tuvieron en la gestación de esta clase, el empeño visionario que pusieron para que la obra se realizara y sobre todo debo agradecerles la benevolencia con que juzgaron mis méritos y capacidades al pensar que fuera yo quien pudiera profesarla.

Trataré de hacerme digno de esta confianza que en

mí depositaron todos ellos.

12. *Op. cit.* p. 12.

En la Historia de la Medicina interesa tanto el más simple elemento narrativo como el más valioso documento bibliográfico.

Hay en ella una mezcla de leyenda y de historia; hay elementos místicos y experimentales; hay componentes artísticos, casi diríamos estéticos, a la vez que factores del más puro cientismo.

No podemos desperdiciar ni los unos ni los otros.

.   .   .   .   .

Así la Historia de la Medicina viene a constituir la más alta cátedra de ética y uno de los más poderosos e innegables factores de progreso científico.

13. Juan Marin. *El problema sexual y sus nuevas fórmulas sociales.* Editorial Nascimento, Santiago: 1937, 275 pages.

14. Juan Marin. *Educación sexual y matrimonio controlado.* Imprenta Andrés Bello, Valparaíso: 1934.

15. *El problema. . . .* pp. 14-15.

Nos damos perfecta cuenta de que el tema que nos proponemos desarrollar es uno de aquéllos más escabrosos que puedan ser dilucidados desde las páginas de un libro ante ese inmenso auditorio mudo que es el público lector. Es tan fácil ser mal interpretado, mal comprendido y mal juzgado. Pero nuestra doble calidad de médico y de sondeador de culturas nos permite desde luego invocar una mayor benevolencia a la vez que manejarnos con mayor confianza tal vez que otros dentro de la cuestión.

.   .   .   .   .

Por eso, sin temores escribimos estas páginas.

16. *Op. cit.* pp. 12-13.

La ascensión del acto carnal hacia la representación intelectual del amor, la simbología mítica creada en torno a este fenómeno fisiológico, constituyen la más hermosa escala construida por los hombres, la verdadera Torre de Babel de las leyendas iniciáticas.

17. *Op. cit.* p. 14.

En el campo biológico no somos materialistas puros ni espiritualistas quintaesenciados. Creemos que ya no caben distingos entre materia y espíritu, entre lo físico y lo psíquico.

18. *Op. cit.* p. 15.

Nuestras soluciones para el agudo problema en materia giran alrededor de dos tópicos fundamentales: *la educación sexual y* la reforma de la actual concepción y legislación sobre el matrimonio, para llegar a lo que denominaremos *matrimonio controlado.*

19. *Op. cit.* p. 56.

These ten points are so fundamental that we copy them verbatim:

La Liga Mundial para la Reforma Sexual ha sintetizado el espíritu y las finalidades de la nueva moral del sexo. Sus postulados son: 1. Igualdad de derechos de la mujer con el hombre, tanto en el terreno político como en el económico y sexual. 2. Liberación del matrimonio y muy en especial del divorcio, de la tutela de la Iglesia y del Estado. 3. Concepción a voluntad para que el parto sea deliberado. 4. Mejora de la raza por divulgación de los conocimientos eugenésicos. 5. Protección a la madre soltera; reconocimiento de la igualdad completa de los hijos legítimos e ilegítimos. 6. Justa apreciación de los estados intersexuales, tanto en el hombre como en la mujer. 7. Prevención de la prostitución y las enfermedades venéreas. 8. Considerar las perturbaciones del instinto sexual como fenómenos patalógicos y no como crímenes u ofensas a la colectividad. 9. Un nuevo derecho sexual, por el que sólo se consideren criminales aquellos actos sexuales que infrinjan las garantías humanas: entre adultos responsables llevados a cabo por mutuo consentimiento, se considerarán como asuntos personales de dichos adultos. 10. Educación sexual sistemática.

20. *Op. cit.* p. 270.

Pondremos fin con las hermosas palabras de Jiménez de Asúa:

"Cuando en un mañana —¿hasta cuando lejano? — se hayan barrido las trabas que ahora nos ligan a convencionalismos formalistas, el mejoramiento de las razas se cumplirá automáticamente. Y no sólo en su aspecto de vigor animal, sino en sus cualidades del espíritu.

"Tras de aquellas frentes perfectas de hombres y mujeres, puros, sin ignorancia e innobles perjuicios, se forjará, sereno el ideal."

21. Juan Marin. *Ensayos freudianos.* Zig-Zag, Santiago: 1939, 287 pages.

22. *Op. cit. Introducción.* p. 35.

Hemos querido reunir en este libro algunos trabajos dispersos sobre temas médicos, históricos o artísticos, que — en su mayoría — tienen alguna relación con el freudismo.

No pretendemos ser originales sino en mínimo grado: es nuestra obra, más que nada, un intento de difusión de contenidos culturales.

Las doctrinas freudianas nos han servido casi siempre como instrumento para el estudio de cada tema. Otras veces, la interpretación psicoanalítica ha sido la base de nuestro trabajo.

En todo caso, el título "ENSAYOS FREUDIANOS" y el espíritu que sopla sobre sus páginas aspiran principalmente a significar un homenaje al sabio cuya vida y cuya obra se han ceñido en forma tan sobria como ejemplar, a la sentencia del intérprete de Zarathustra, que nos sirve de epígrafe.

Llegue este libro hasta el silencioso retiro del Maestro llevándole unos jirones de nuestra ferviente admiración.

(Note: Freud was dying of cancer in London, England at the time of the publication of *Ensayos freudianos.*)

23. We have been perhaps a bit too technical in our discussions of Dr. Marín's *Ensayos* . . . ; it is well to insist again that our interest in this volume, as in all the others, is in its literary aspects or in its application to Dr. Marín's literary theories. We have pointed out, from time to time, his tendency to accept idealism rather than materialism or realism. There seem to be three main points in Freudism that our author accepts as Freud's contribution to literary practice: incest, cannibalism, and violence. In *Orestes y yo* and in certain chapters of *Ensayos* . . . , i.e. "Restif de la Bretonne" and "Byron y el incesto" (see pages 175 ff.), incest is discussed. In *Naufragio* we have direct references to cannibalism, and, in spite of Dr. Marín's dislike of violence, he makes use of it in *Paralelo* . . . , and in several of his short stories.

24. *Op. cit.* pp. 51-69.

We choose a few passages from *Ensayos* . . . that give us a bit of Dr. Marín's philosophy of creative art. (p. 51.)

Nuestra información de los numerosos libros y ensayos, hasta ahora consagrados a esta transcendental cuestión de la creación artística, nos muestra cómo los hombres siempre han aparecido divididos en dos grandes grupos de doctrinas para explicarla: los espiritualistas y los materialistas.

. . . . .

Porque al fin de cuentas no es otra la verdadera cuestión que se plantea cuando se discute la ubicación del escritor dentro de la sociedad, cuando se habla del arte con contenido social en oposición al "arte por el arte", al "torremarfilismo", al arte de evasión, etc.

It is, however, on page 68 that Dr. Marin accepts the idea that art to be eternal must have a purpose other than merely being art:

El filósofo Oswald Spengler escribió: "El arte por el arte es sólo un deporte." Y Upton Sinclair expresó, a su vez: "El arte por el arte es la doctrina de artistas desorientados, es cobardía y degeneración."

Note: These quotations from the chapter "Génesis y proceso del arte" (Beginning and Evolution of Art) are fundamental. (This chapter was published also in the outstanding critico-literary journal *Atenea,* December 1936, p. 138 ff.)

25. *Op. cit.* pp. 95-111.

Although the sub-title of this chapter suggests that "The Fetishism of the Foot" forms the main subject, there are hints of incest. (See note 23 above.) Whether or not some of the women with whom Restif associated were really his daughters, he often referred to them as such.

26. *Op. cit.* pp. 129-136. "Disección psicoanalítica de Leon Tolstoy."

Dr. Marin continued to respect and admire Tolstoy as a novelist but did not hesitate to psychoanalyze him. A few short quotations will point out some of Dr. Marin's own attitudes as well as to remind us that the author of *War and Peace* was not the saint that many considered him to be.

Tolstoy, in spite of being somewhat of a *malade imaginaire,* who called for doctors at the slightest physical upset, lost no opportunity to criticize adversely the medical profession: (page 129)

Es curiosa e interesante la situación planteada entre el apóstol ruso y la Medicina. Durante toda su vida el Conde novelista no perdió oportunidad de zaherir, de rebajar y de combatir a los médicos y a su ciencia, en términos que no tuvieron la gracia picante de los de Moliére, ni la agudeza incisiva de los de Voltaire, ni el ático sabor de los de Anatole France, ni la mordacidad satírica de los de G. B. Shaw.

27. *Op. cit.* p. 135.

Dr. Marin cites such penetrating critics as Thomas Mann, Ossipov, and Turgunef but it is probably this summary of what Adler has said that explains the reasons for some of the Count's acts:

> En él se hace evidente más que en ningún otro, ese sentimiento que Adler ha llamado de "pan-superioridad", y que empuja al hombre a constituirse en Dios, y en un Dios único, sin rivales. La escenificación de este complejo la encontramos en aquellas audiencias que concedía a mendigos y mujiks, sentado bajo la sombra de un añoso olmo en el parque de su castillo. Allí estaba muy bien en su papel de "Dios".

28. *Op. cit.* p. 136.

In the last paragraph of this chapter Dr. Marin explains, without excusing the Count, how contemporary psychologists have debunked the count-mujik:

> . . . y la medicina tan injustamente valpuleada por Tolstoy, el autodidacta y el vegetariano, desciende de su altar al "Santo de Yasnaia-Poliana" y lo tiende blandamente sobre la mesa de disección. Con los textos de Freud, de Rank, de Lavastine, etc., en la mano, los médicos de hoy nos ofrecen elegantemente, junto al enorme cuerpo yacente, una brillante lección de patalogía mental.

29. *Atenea.* No. 138. December 1936, pp. 264-289. (Also note listing of this essay in Dr. John P. Dyson's *La evolución de la crítica literaria en Chile.* Santiago: 1965, p. 146.)

Chapter VII

1. "Juan Jacobo Rousseau." *El Mercurio.* (Unless otherwise stated, *El Mercurio* will mean *El Mercurio de Santiago:* Chile.) Oct. 18, 1962.

> Hoy día la influencia de Rousseau es muy reducida. Tal vez los últimos brotes "rousseaunianos" los ha dado Tolstoy en Rusia, Gandhi en la India y Thoreau en la Nueva Inglaterra. Pero es evidente que sus ideas ejercieron una terrible e incalculable influencia en los hombres de la Revolución Francesa: . . . .

2. "H. D. Thoreau." *Op. cit.* May 28, 1962.

> . . . nunca hubiera creído él que sería un día objeto de homenajes como los que su patria acaba de rendirle. Su lección—ejemplarizada por su vida misma—fue una lección de olvido, de retiro y de humildad. Pero siempre tuvo una fe profunda en el destino del hombre: "se ne-

cesita no ser cristiano para comprender en toda su sublime belleza la vida de Cristo," escribió Thoreau . . . "La luz que alumbra nuestros ojos es en verdad obscuridad para nosotros. El día amanece sólo para aquél que ya está despierto. Y el día es no sólo el amanecer. El sol es apenas una estrella de la mañana."

3. "Upton Sinclair." *Op. cit.* June 13, 1962.

Literariamente hablando, Sinclair es un hermano de Jack London y de John Dos Passos, aunque tal vez no haya tenido una influencia tan marcada como la de estos dos sobre los escritores latinoamericanos de nuestra generación. . . . Recordamos que, influenciados por *La Selva,* nosotros iniciamos uno de nuestros poemas titulado "Yankilandia" con estos versos:

> En Chicago chorizos de a mil dólares
> Libertades de piedra en Nueva York. . . .

. . . . . .

. . . vegetariano estricto, se alimenta más que nada de frutas producidas en su propia granja. . . .

Al enfrentar a los periodistas con motivo de recibir su homenaje, Upton Sinclair no ha ocultado que su intelecto sigue siendo ágil y vivaz. "Yo sigo siendo un socialista como siempre lo fui, pero mi esposa prefiere ahora decir que mi socialismo se llama *democracia industrial* y yo no la objeto" y agrega: "Sin duda los comunistas nos han hecho duro el camino a nosotros los socialistas."

4. "William Faulkner." *El Mercurio,* July 14, 1962.

Faulkner dijo una vez de sí mismo: "Soy sólo un escritor, no un literato." Y ésta es una de las mayores verdades que dijo en su vida, pues nada hay en su estilo literario que haga grata o brillante su lectura. Por el contrario, se complacía en erizar de dificultades el camino del lector; su estilo es oscuro, desaliñado, inconexo, repetitivo, quebrado y hasta muchas veces incorrecto; en todo caso es un estilo difícil. La frase se hace en ocasiones tan larga como la de Henry James, con el agravante de que mientras en Henry James ella es larga y tersa, en Faulkner se retuerce, se quiebra y se alimbica hasta el absurdo. . . .

5. *Loc. cit.*

Con tan inmenso lastre artístico ¿cuál es entonces la virtud que hace de Faulkner uno de los autores más leídos, más traducidos y más imitados hoy en el mundo?

6. *Loc. cit.*

La respuesta es doble; en primer lugar, el tema sureño
. . . y el vigor del relato.

7. "Ernest Hemingway." *La Semana.* Guayaquil, July 22, 1961.

Nunca preguntes por quién repican las campanas,
repican por ti.

Así escribió Ernest Hemingway en el epígrafe de su
dramática y difundida novela sobre la guerra civil española.
Hoy, mientras nosotros escribimos estas líneas, las campanas de la pequeña iglesia de Sun Valley, en Idaho,
estarán repicando por este hombre que nunca quiso hacerse
la pregunta trascendental, no por miedo ¡qué nunca lo
tuvo! — sino porque bien conoció la respuesta.

. . . . .

Hemingway ha puesto fin a todo en la mañana del 3
de julio en su casa de campo del Valle del Sol entre las
altas montañas de Idaho.

8. *Loc. cit.* (Dr. Marin points out the personal style of Hemingway.)

Siendo muy joven encontró en Paris, en la inolvidable
Gertrude Stein, una maestra y una amiga que le ayudó
a encontrar el camino. Pero después el camino se lo labró
él por sí mismo, volcando ideas y bellezas sobre la con-
ciencia de los hombres. El creó un estilo literario que nada
debe a su maestra Gertrude Stein, pero que sí encontró
en cambio muchos imitadores. La frase corta, seca, dura
y anti-romántica es cosa suya. El diálogo de estilo periodís-
tico, breve, entrecortado y sintético es también suyo. Los lar-
gos silencios de *El viejo y el mar* son también cosa muy suya.

9. "John Steinbeck Premio Nobel de Literatura."

Es curioso notar que todos ellos (Sinclair Lewis, Pearl
Buck, Eugene O'Neill, William Faulkner y Ernest Hemingway) tienen en mayor o menor grado un sentido de
inconformidad en sus escritos, un soplo de rebeldía y un
fuerte contenido de crítica social. En este aspecto Steinbeck
más que ninguno.

. . . . .

. . . Combina una especie de humorismo picaresco como
en *Tortilla Flat* con la cálida ternura y la muy humana
compasión de *Las viñas de la ira.*

. . . . .

Again we read:

En todas sus obras Steinbeck se ha mostrado como un

novelista del tipo proletario y un naturalista de gran objectividad, pero su naturalismo está empregnado de una gran ternura por los oprimidos y por los desamparados, semejante a Gorki y los rusos del siglo pasado.

10. *Loc. cit.*

Se ha cumplido un acto de justicia al premiar a este novelista de 62 años cuya obra ha marcado ya una huella profunda en la literatura de su país. Hace pocos meses al ser entrevistado por un diario dejó entrever que la idea de la muerte comienza a perfilarse en su horizonte psicológico: "Nada hay que limpie tanto como morir. Si usted se queda mucho tiempo, se aburren con usted. Y yo sinceramente pienso que me he adherido a la vida un poco más de lo necesario."

Estas palabras parecieron un eco de aquellas pronunciadas por Eugene O'Neill también en sus últimos años y quisieron preludiar el cruce del umbral que esta vez le ha sido abierto con mano de oro por el Premio Nobel: el umbral de la fama y de la perennidad.

11. "Boris Pasternak." *El Mercurio.* June 26, 1961.

Pasternak amaba a Rusia tal como todos los seres humanos amamos a nuestras patrias. Y tal vez más que los demás, porque él la había visto sufrir y había luchado por su redención. El doctor Zivago tiene algo de religioso en su íntima naturaleza. Algo que lo hace un testamento moral, un legado ejemplar para la posteridad. "He querido mostrar la vida tal como ella es, en toda su riqueza e intensidad," escribió Pasternak. El nunca quiso que su obra fuera un panfleto político, ni menos pudo siquiera soñar que habría de transformarse en una de las obras más polémicas de este siglo.

12. *Loc. cit.* (We presume, although Dr. Marin does not say so, that the following translation was made by him, probably from the English or Italian.)

Héme aquí perdido como una bestia feroz en un encierro,
en alguna parte del mundo hay gentes, hay libertad
        y hay luz,
detrás de mí sólo escucho el ruido de la jauría
y no hay escape para mí. . . .
Pero, ¿qué cosa tan mala, que crímen he cometido,
        yo a quien se llama asesino y villano?
Yo, cuyo solo delito es haber hecho llorar al mundo

entero sobre las bellezas de mi tierra?
En todo caso, ya estoy muy cerca de la tumba
y creo que el tiempo llegará
en que el espíritu del bien habrá de conquistar
la realidad y la infamia.

13. *Loc. cit.* (Dr. Marin returns to the novel.)

. . . Su libro (i.e. Pasternak's novel *El doctor Zivago*) ha sido leído por millones de seres humanos que han encontrado en él arte y emoción, y sobre todo una gran dosis de poesía, de esa poesía auténtica que es como el aliento de la tierra y como la respiración del alma de los hombres. Pasternak trascendió de sí mismo. En su libro *El doctor Zivago* sobrepasó las fronteras de Rusia y llegó a ser parte del bagaje espiritual de toda la humanidad.

14. "Poesía." *El Mercurio.* Octuber 30, 1962.

. . . Porque si ha de llegar el fin, en forma de una bomba "A" o de una bomba "H" que nos envíe el señor Khruschev, lo mejor que pueda ocurrirnos es que nos encuentre recitando o escuchando poemas.

15. *Loc. cit.*

No hay paralelismo alguno entre el vigor de la novela y el teatro en los Estados Unidos y la débil y anémica figura que traza su poesía. Se diría que con esos gigantes que fueron Poe y Whitman se agotaron todas las reservas de inspiración que habían sido asignadas a esta parte del mundo; no dejaron nada para los demás.

BIBLIOGRAPHIES

The following pages, 207 ff., contain bibliographies that we hope will be helpful to persons interested in carrying on investigations concerning Dr. Marin and his writings. Although these are listed in *CONTENTS* we repeat them here:

Selected Bibliographies

A. *BOOK LENGTH PUBLICATIONS BY JUAN MARIN*, listed chronologically.

La tiro-toxicosis y su tratamiento quirúgico (Thyroid Toxicosis and its Surgical Treatment). (Tesis de licenciatura) Santiago, Chile: Soc. Imp. i Lit. Universo. 1921, 150 pages.

Looping. (Poems) Santiago: Nascimento, 1929, 118 pages.

Clínicas y maestros en Inglaterra y Francia (Clinics and Professors in England and France). (Notas de viaje) Valparaíso: Ediciones Boletín médico de Chile, 1930, 133 pages.

Margarita, el aviador y el médico (Margaret, the Aviator, and the Doctor). (Novel) Prologue by Hernán del Solar. Santiago: Zig-Zag, 1932, 96 pages.

La muerte de Julián Aranda (The Death of Julian Aranda). (Novelette) Santiago: Zig-Zag, 1933, 54 pages.

Poliedro médico (Medical Miscellany). (Essays) Valparaíso: Editorial Chilena, 1933, 200 pages.

Alas sobre el mar (Wings Over the Sea). (Short Stories) Prologue by Salvador Reyes. Santiago: Julio Walton, 1934, 242 pages.

Aquarium. (Poems) Illustrated by Pedro Olmos. Santiago: Editorial Julio Walton, 1934, 26 pages.*

Hacia la nueva moral (Toward a New Morality). (Essays) Valparaíso: Editorial Medicina Moderna, 1934, 36 pages.*

Un avión volaba (A Plane Was Flying). (Novel) Prologue by Ernesto Montenegro. Santiago: Editorial Ercilla, 1935, 187 pages.

Paralelo 53 sur (Parallel 53 South). (Novel) Prologue by Emilio Rodríguez Mendoza. Santiago: Nascimento, 1936, 220 pages.

———————— (Second Edition). Prologue by Francisco Ferrándiz Alborz. Santiago. Nascimento, 1941, 213 pages.

———————— (Third Edition). Santiago: Nascimento, 1955, 208 pages.

El infierno azul y blanco (The Blue and White Hell). (Argentine edition of *Paralelo 53 sur*) Prologue by Elías Castelnuovo. Buenos Aires: Editorial Claridad, 1937, 174 pages.

O infierno azul e branco (Portuguese edition of *El infierno azul y blanco*). Translated by Francisco Quintal. Prologue by Ferrándiz Alborz. Lisboa: Livararia Renascenza, 1939, 223 pages.

* Because of their special significance these items are included with "Book Length Publications."

Paralelo 53 sur (Translated to Yugoslave by Rajna Djurdjev). Beograd: Editorial Prosveta, 1958, 138 pages.

El secreto del Dr. Baloux (The Secret of Dr. Baloux). (Novel) Prologue by Augusto d'Halmar. Santiago: Editorial Ercilla, 1936, 202 pages.*

El problema sexual y sus nuevas fórmulas sociales (The Problem of Sex and its New Sociological Formulas). (Essays) Santiago: Nascimento, 1937, 273 pages.

Ensayos freudianos de la medicina, de la historia y del arte (Freudian Essays Concerning Medicine, History, and Art). Prologue by Humberto Salvador. Santiago: Zig-Zag, 1938, 267 pages.

Naufragio (Shipwreck). (Novel) Santiago: Editorial Zig-Zag, 1939, 93 pages.

Orestes y yo (Orestes and I). (Novel) Prologue by Dr. José Belbey. Santiago: Nascimento, 1939, 220 pages.

Orestes y yo (Drama en tres actos). (Drama) Introduction by Jorge Carrera Andrade. Tokio, Japón: Ediciones Asia-América, 1940, 64 pages.

Orestes and I (Play in Three Acts). Translated from Spanish by Richard P. Butrick. Tokyo, Japan: Ediciones Asia-América, 1941, 66 pages.

El emperador Kwang Hsü (Emperor Kwang Hsü). (Drama) Tokio, Japón: Ediciones Asia-América, 1941, 138 pages.

Emperor Kwang Hsü. (Drama) Translated from Spanish by Richard P. Butrick. Tokyo, Japan: Ediciones Asia-América, 1941, 138 pages.

Flames in the Darkness. (Novel) Translation from Spanish of the novel *Naufragio* by Richard P. Butrick. Tokyo, Japan: Ediciones Asia-América, 1941, 81 pages.

China: Lao-Tszé, Confucio, Buda (China: Lao Tszé, Confucius, Buddha). (Religio-philosophical treatise) Buenos Aires: Editorial Espasa Calpe, 1944, 454 pages.

El Tibet misterioso y sus lamas (Mysterious Tibet and Her Lamas). (Religio-philosophical Treatise) Santiago: Nascimento, 1944, 172 pages.

Viento negro (Black Wind). Santiago: Nascimento, 1944, 255 pages.
----------------------- (Second edition of above). Santiago: Zig-Zag, 1960, 199 pages.

El alma de China; su arte, su literatura, sus ideas (The Soul of China; Her Art, Her Literature, Her Ideas). Buenos Aires: Editorial Claridad, 1945, 441 pages.

Mesa de mah-jong; una crónica de China (The Mah-jong Table, A

* This edition of *El secreto* . . . included a few other stories and a number of critical opinions. *El secreto* . . . occupies only 76 pages of the publication.

Chronicle of China). Buenos Aires: Editorial Emecé, 1948, 363 pages.

Cuentos de viento y agua (Stories of the Air and Sea). Prologue by Juan Felipe Toruño. Santiago: Nascimento, 1949, 235 pages.

Lao-Tszé o El universalismo mágico (Lao-Tszé or Magical Universalism). (Religio-philosophical Treatise) Buenos Aires: Editorial Espasa Calpe, 1953, 166 pages.

Confucio o El humanismo didactizante (Confucius or Didactic Humanism). (Religio-philosophical Treatise) Buenos Aires: Editorial Espasa Calpe, 1953, 147 pages.

Muerte en Shanghai (Death in Shanghai). (Novel) Prologue by José Sanz y Díaz. Madrid: Editorial Rollán, 1953, 93 pages.

Naufragio y otros cuentos (Shipwreck and Other Stories). (A novel and two novelettes are added to the original edition of *Naufragio.*) Prologue by José Sanz y Díaz and epilogues by Jorge Carrera Andrade and Absalón Baldovinos. Santiago: Editorial Zig-Zag, 1953, 209 pages.

Buda o la negación del mundo (Buddha or the Denial of the World). (Religio-philosophical Treatise) Buenos Aires: Editorial Espasa Calpe, 1954, 226 pages.

El Egipto de los Faraones (The Egypt of the Pharaohs). (Travel and Interpretation) Santiago: Editorial Zig-Zag, 1954; second edition 1955; third edition 1963, 378 pages.

La India eterna (Eternal India). (Travel and Interpretation) Santiago: Editorial Zig-Zag, 1954; second edition 1956, 474 pages.

B. *SHORTER PUBLICATIONS BY JUAN MARIN: PAMPHLETS, LECTURES, REPRINTS, ETC.* (Listed alphabetically)

Acerca del carcinoma del próstata. Santiago: Imprenta Siglo XX, 1951, 15 pages.

Algunas consideraciones acerca del secreto profesional y de la medicina. Santiago: Imprenta y Litografía le Blanc, 1931, 20 pages.

Angulos psicológicos en la vida y obras de José Batres Montúfar. San Salvador, El Salvador: Imprenta Nacional, 1945, 24 pages.

La aviación como factor de enfermedades. (Patología de Aviación) Santiago: (Reprint from *Revista médica de Chile),* Jan. 1929, 7 pages.

Un caso de hemoglobinuria paroxística en un heredo-luético. (con el doctor E. W. Coutts) Buenos Aires: *Revista médica latino-americana,* Aug. 1925, No. 119, 5 pages.

Chinese jade. Cairo, Egypt: Editorial Al-Hilal, 1948, 29 pages.

The Chinese Dragon. Bombay, India: *The Aryan Path,* March 1952, No. 3, Vol. XXIII, 12 pages.

JUAN MARIN

El derrumbe del cielo. Concepción: *Atenea,* Vol. 106, No. 322, pp. 60-78. (Also San Salvador, El Salvador: *La estrella de Centroamérica,* April 1952, 9 pages.)

L'Emotivité et la névrose de guerre. Paris: *Bulletin Internacionale,* Jan. 1936, 10 pages.

Los fenómenos de la emoción ante la filosofía y la medicina. Santiago: Imprenta de la Armada, 1931, 14 pages.

La hernia como enfermedad profesional proveniente de un accidente del servicio. Buenos Aires: *Revista médica latino-americana,* Imprenta Mercantali, April 1929, No. 163, 10 pages.

Héroes anónimos. (Short Story) Santiago: *La Nación,* Oct. 7, 1921.

Hielos magallánicos en un campo de concentración de Shanghai. (Short Story) Santiago: *La Hora,* May 3, 1945.

Hipócrates y el hipocratismo. Valparaíso: *Medicina moderna,* Dec. 1952, 11 pages.

Informe prestado a la superioridad naval por el Capitán de Corbeta cirujano Dr. Juan Marín R. sobre observaciones profesionales recogidos en su viaje a EE. UU. de N.A. Valparaíso: *Revista de sanidad naval,* 1945, 9 pages.

Introducción al estudio de la Historia de la Medicina. (Lección inaugural dictada en la Universidad de Chile el 25 de abril de 1932.) Santiago, Chile: Imprenta de la Armada. 1932, 27 pages.

La ley de seguro social. San Salvador, El Salvador: *Publicaciones del ministerio de Cultura,* 1945, 30 pages.

The OAS and Education. New York: *Teachers College Record,* Oct. 1963, Vol. 65, No. 1, pp. 11-16.

El origen de la medicina hipocrática. Valparaíso: *Medicina moderna,* Oct. 1959, 15 pages.

Paracelso, la medicina y la magia. Valparaíso: *Medicina moderna,* July 1932, No. 12, 13 pages.

Los pies vendados de la mujer china y el fetichismo del pie. Lima, Peru: 1941, 9 pages.

El problema del hijo frente a la clase obrera (Cartilla sanitaria dedicada a los padres y a los que van a serlo). Santiago: Imprenta Santiago, 1925, 18 pages.

La retención aguda de orina de causas extra-vesículas. Valparaíso: *Medicina moderna,* April 1932, No. 31, 17 pages.

La sífilis—su influencia en el progreso nacional. Santiago: Imprenta Santiago, 1925, 12 pages.

Tríptico china, Estratto de Il Marco Polo. Sciangai: Anno III, No. 11, Aprile, 1942, 4 pages.

Una supuesta "Tumba de Cristo" en Cachemira, India. San José, Costa

Rica: *Repertorio Americano,* Mar. 19, 1950, Vol. XLVI, No. 6, p. 4.

Viaje en el "Hurricane" (Voyage on the "Hurricane"). (Short Story) Santiago: *El Mercurio,* Mar. 22, 1964. (Also published in Los Angeles, Cal.: *La Opinión,* May 10, 1964.)*

C. SECONDARY SOURCES

Anderson Imbert, Enrique. *Literatura hispanoamericana.* Vol. II. México-Buenos Aires: Fondo de cultura económica, 1961.

Balseiro, José A. *Expresión de hispanoamérica* (Segunda Serie). San Juan, P. R.: Instituto de Cultura Puertorriqueña, 1963, 207 pages.

------------------------ *Paralelo 53 sur.* Santiago: *El Mercurio,* Dec. 19, 1964.

Díaz Arrieta, Hernán (Pseud. *Alone*). *Historia personal de la literatura chilena.* (Segunda edición). Santiago: Nascimento, 1954, 669 pages.

Durand, Luis. *Gente de mi tiempo.* Santiago: Nascimento, 1953, 227 pages.

González y Contreras, Gilberto. *Un estudio de la obra de Juan Marín.* Tokio, Japón: Ediciones Asia-América, 1940, 25 pages.

Huneeus, Sergio. *Hombres y lugares.* Quito, Ecuador: Casa de Cultura, 1963, 276 pages.

------------------------ *Juan Marín y La India eterna.* Concepción, Chile: *Atenea,* Vol. CXXVI. No. 372, Sept.-Oct. 1956, pp. 72-79.

Lindo, Hugo. *La más reciente obra de Juan Marín.* San Salvador, El Salvador: *Síntesis,* Año 1, No. 8, Nov. 1954, pp. 47-51.

Merino Reyes, Luis. *Juan Marín, cuentista, médico, novelista.* Washington, D. C. (OAS): *Interamerican Review of Bibliography,* Jan.-Mar., 1964. No. 1, pp. 3-20.

Montecinos, Manuel. *El mar en la literatura chilena.* Santiago: Editorial del Pacífico, 1958, 240 pages.

Montes, Hugo y Julio Orlandini. *Historia de la literatura chilena.* Santiago: Editorial del Pacífico, 1958, 338 pages.

Sabella, Andrés. *Juan Marín y la nueva inspiración.* Santiago: *El Mercurio,* Feb. 9, 1946.

Sarah C., Roberto. *Juan Marín, aventurero: sus "Cuentos de viento y agua."* Concepción: *Atenea,* No. 321, pp. 331-332.

Silva Castro, Raúl. *Panarama de la novela chilena.* Santiago: Editorial Universitaria, 1961, 570 pages.

Toruño, Juan Felipe. *Los desterrados.* San Salvador, El Salvador: Tipografía "La Luz" de *Diario latino,* 1938, 219 pages.

------------------------. *Poesía y poetas de América; trayecto en ámbitos*

* For lists "A" and "B" above, we are indebted to Frank P. Hebblethwaite's *Bibliography* published in the OAS magazine *Inter-American Review of Bibliography,* Jan.-Mar. 1964, Vol. XIV, No. 1, pp. 17-20.

fisonomías y posiciones. San Salvador, El Salvador, Imprenta Funes, 1945, 434 pages.

D. *UNPUBLISHED STUDIES CONCERNING JUAN MARIN*
Note: *These studies, along with others not dealing directly with Juan Marin, are listed in EDICIONES DE LA BIBLIOTECA NACIONAL, DIRECCION DE BIBLIOTECAS, ARCHIVOS Y MUSEOS, BIBLIOGRAFIA DE LAS MEMORIAS DE GRADO SOBRE LITERATURA CHILENA (1919-1967) prepared by Thomas MacHale. We have found these eight quite significant. These essays may be compared to Senior Theses required by some colleges and universities in the United States. They vary widely in scholarship and critical value.*

Armijo Rojas, Marina. *Criollismo e imaginismo en el cuento chileno.*
Durand Muñoz, José Luis. *Tierra del fuego en la literatura chilena.*
González Fuensalida, Eugenia. *El cuento chileno en el siglo XX.*
Guerrero, Leoncio. *Homenaje a Juan Marín* (Leído el 17 de noviembre de 1963 en la Sala Valentín Letelier de la Universidad de Chile, Santiago, Chile).
Miranda Sallorenso, Manuel. *Algunos tipos de aventureros en la literatura chilena.*
Paez Boggino, Osvaldo. *La novela de la generación actual.*
Ramírez Fernández, Julio. *Literatura chilena marítima (Bosquejo histórico).*
Reyes Contreras, Marta. *La novela de ambiente social en Chile y la novela hispanoamericana actual.*

E. *SELECTED LIST OF CHILEAN NEWSPAPERS AND MAGAZINES THAT PUBLISHED MISCELLANEOUS WORKS OF JUAN MARIN*
Atenea. (Revista literaria mensual) Concepción, Chile: 1931-39.
Boletín médico de Chile. (Semanal) Valparaíso, Chile: 1936-39.
La clínica. (Revista médica mensual) Santiago: 1926-39.
El diario Austral. (Diario) Temuco: 1937-39.
La hora. (Diario) Santiago: 1939-53.
Lecturas. (Revista literaria mensual) Santiago: 1932.
Letras. (Revista literaria mensual) Cuentos, poemas y artículos literarios. Santiago: 1930.
El magallanes. (Diario) Punta Arenas: 1933-36.
Medicina moderna. (Revista médica mensual) Valparaíso: 1932-38.
El mercurio de Santiago. (Diario) Santiago: 1953-63.
La nación. (Diario) Crónica médica de actualidad. (Signed *Sanín*) Santiago: 1926.
Revista de sanidad naval. (Bi-mensual) Valparaíso: 1931-39.

La Unión. (Diario) Valparaíso: 1938-39.

En viaje. (Revista literaria y general de los Ferrocarriles del Estado, mensual) Santiago: 1953-56.

Vida médica. (Revista médica mensual) Santiago: 1931-32.

Zig-Zag. (Revista literaria-social, semanal) Artículos y crónicas 1939-56; Crítica literaria (Signed *IGOR*) Santiago: 1955.

F. SELECTED LIST OF FOREIGN NEWSPAPERS AND MAGAZINES THAT PUBLISHED MISCELLANEOUS WORKS OF JUAN MARIN
Boletín de la Biblioteca Nacional. San Salvador, El Salvador.
Cuadernos americanos. México, D.F.: México.
Diario de las Américas. Miami, Fla.: USA.
El diario latino. San Salvador, El Salvador.
La gaceta de la prensa española. Madrid, Spain.
Hippocrate. Paris, France.
Marginales. Bruxelles, Belgium.
La nueva democracia. N.Y. USA.
La opinión. Los Angeles, Cal. USA.
El repertorio americano. San José, Costa Rica.
Revue Générale. Bruxelles, Belgium.
La semana. Guayaquil, Ecuador.
Universidad de Antioquia. Medellín, Colombia.

G. SOME IMPORTANT PROLOGUES TO JUAN MARIN'S WORKS.
Belbey, Dr. José. Prologue to *Orestes y yo,* novel.
Carrera Andrade, Jorge. Prologue to *Orestes y yo,* drama.
Castelnuovo, Elías. Prologue to *Infierno azul y blanco.*
Ferrándiz, Alborz. Prologue to *Paralelo 53 sur.*
d'Halmar, Augusto. Prologue to *El secreto del Dr. Baloux.*
Hernán del Solar. Prologue to *Margarita, el aviador y el médico.*
----------------- Prologue to Second edition of above.
Montenegro, Ernesto. Prologue to *Un avión volaba.*
Reyes, Salvador. Prologue to *Alas sobre el mar.*
Rodríguez Mendoza, Emilio. Prologue to *Paralelo 53 sur* (First Edition).
Salvador, Humberto. Prologue to *Ensayos freudianos.*
Sanz y Díaz, José. Prologue to *Naufragio y otros cuentos.*
----------------- Prologue to *Muerte en Shanghai.*

H. SHORT LIST OF WORKS BY JUAN MARIN PUBLISHED IN ANTHOLOGIES AND IN FOREIGN LANGUAGE MAGAZINES
Antología de cuentos contemporáneos. "El hombre de medianoche," Barcelona: Editorial Labor, 1964.
Antología de cuentistas hispanoamericanos. "En el límite," Madrid: M. Aguilar, 1946.

Narradores hispanoamericanos. "Nupcial," Barcelona: Hymsa, 1942.
Siete poetas chilenos. "Mecánica," Buenos Aires: La Carabela, 1948.
Siete cuentos chilenos. "Puerto negro," México: Biblioteca enciclopedia popular, 1945.
Poetas jóvenes de América. "Un ford de frac." Madrid: M. Aguilar, 1930.
Trece relatos hispánicos "El hombre de medianoche." New York: Odyssey Press, 1959.
Short Stories of Latin America. New York: Las Américas, 1963.
The Green Continent. New York: Alfred A. Knopf, 1954.

I. *TRANSLATED TO FRENCH AND PUBLISHED IN BELGUIM*
Marginales. (Revue trimestrielle des idées et des lettres)
"L'Homme fait de musique" and "L'epreuve de la corde."

J. *LIST OF CRITICS WHOSE WORKS HAVE BEEN CONSULTED WITHOUT DIRECT QUOTATIONS BEING USED*
Andrade Coello, Alejandro; Arauz de Robles, Carlos; Barella, Carlos; Barrios, Eduardo; Beals, Carlton; Billa Garrido, Augustín; Boye Soto, Enrique; Carrera Andrade, Jorge; Carill, Adelina de, (de Güiraldes); Castro, Ernesto; Chávez, José María; Correa, Carlos Réné; Cvitanic, Juan V.; Falconi, Villagómez, J. A.; Falgaroille, Adolphe de; Fuenzalida, Hector; Gálvez, Alejandro; García Oldini, Fernando; Gémas, Oscar; Guerra, Gregorio; Guzmán, Oscar; Heliodoro Valle, Rafael; Hubner, Manuel Eduardo; Iduarte, Andrés; Jarnés, Benjamín; Jobet, Julio César; Kamarenko, José; Labarca Garat, Gustavo; Lafourcade, Enrique; Lazarte, Juan; Lillo, Victoriano; Loveluck, Juan; Mata, G. Humberto; Miomandre, Francis de; Mistral, Gabriela; Ortega, Serafín; Pereda Valdés, Ildefonso; Pillement, Georges; Pinilla, Norberto; Peña, Aquilino; Préndez Saldías, Carlos; Guinzio, Camilo; Rehione, Dr. Humberto; Rivera Flores, Gustavo; Rosel, Milton; Sánchez, Alberto Luis; Sanín Rivera, E.; Monserrat, Santiago; Santiván, Fernando; Schwarzenberger, L. Julio; Smilnoff, Marcos; Vandercammen, Edmond; Vega, Manuel; Vidart, Daniel D.; Villagarrida, Augustín.

K. *BIOGRAPHICAL PUBLICATIONS THAT LIST JUAN MARIN*
The Authors and Writers Who's Who. Barket Peerage, London.
Hombres y Lugares. Casa de Cultura Ecuatoriana. Quito, Ecuador: 1963. (See pages 51-59) "Juan Marín y la India eterna."
2000 Biografías Breves Mundiales de Todos los Tiempos. Libros de América. Hanover, Pa.: EE. UU., 1963.
Who's Who in Latin America. (Third Edition) A. N. Marquis, Chicago.
Who's Who in the South and Southwest. Marquis, Chicago: 1950.
World Biography. New York, N. Y.: 1948.

Indices

Two indices are provided: General Index explanation:

a) The names *Juan Marin* and *doña Milena Luksic de Marin* do not normally appear in this index.

b) Geographical and historical terms are usually omitted.

c) Because a special index for *Juan Marin's* works is provided, these are not indexed in this list.

d) If a term occurs very frequently, only the most important references are listed.

e) The General Notes are indexed here.

GENERAL INDEX OF PROPER NAMES

215

SPECIAL INDEX OF JUAN MARIN'S WRITINGS

*Numbers between parenthesis indicate more important entries.

222

Post publication changes (Errata)

Page 12, line 1 ....Universalismo *read* Universismo
  (See also page 114, line 1; page 209, line 5, and page 223, line 4)
Page 22, line 16 ....1956 *read* 1955
Page 22, line 33 ....Santiago *read* Valparaiso
Page 207, line 9 ....1930 *read* 1931
Page 208, line 19 ....1941 *read* 1940
Page 209, line 7 ....1953 *read* 1952
Page 209, line 25 ....1954 *read* 1956
Page 209, line 28 ....acerca del *read* acerca de la
Page 209, line 28 ....1951 *read* 1931
Page 210, line 15 ....1952 *read* 1932
Page 210, line 16 ....prestado *read* presentado
Page 210, line 19 ....1945 *read* 1937
Page 210, line 28 ....1959 *read* 1938
Page 210, line 35 ....1925 *read* 1923
Page 210, line 40 ....china *read* chino
Page 211, line 12 ....Nascimento *read* Zig-Zag
Page 212, line 28 ....1931-39 *read* 1931-62
Page 212, line 30 ....1926-39 *read* 1926-29